# Fiber Channel and SAN Networks: A Complete Implementation Guide

James Relington

# DEDICATION

To those who seek knowledge, inspiration, and new perspectives—
may this book be a companion on your journey, a spark for curiosity,
and a reminder that every page turned is a step toward discovery.

# AKNOWLEDGEMENTS

I would like to express my deepest gratitude to everyone who contributed to the creation of this book. To my colleagues and mentors, your insights and expertise have been invaluable. A special thank you to my family and friends for their unwavering support and encouragement throughout this journey.

# Introduction to Fiber Channel and SAN Networks

Fiber Channel (FC) and Storage Area Networks (SAN) are fundamental components in modern data centers, playing a pivotal role in managing and transferring large volumes of data at high speeds. Fiber Channel technology was developed in the 1980s as a high-speed data transfer protocol specifically designed for storage networks. Over the years, it has become a cornerstone of storage solutions, providing the necessary infrastructure to enable efficient data access, high availability, and robust performance across large enterprise environments. SAN networks, on the other hand, are specialized networks that connect servers and storage devices, allowing them to communicate with each other at high speeds. This chapter introduces the core concepts of Fiber Channel and SAN networks, explaining how they work and why they are essential for businesses that require large-scale, reliable, and efficient storage systems.

At the heart of any SAN infrastructure is Fiber Channel, a high-performance network protocol that is specifically optimized for data storage. Unlike traditional Ethernet, which was designed primarily for general data traffic, Fiber Channel is built with storage traffic in mind. It offers high throughput, low latency, and the ability to transfer large amounts of data over long distances, which are all crucial characteristics for enterprise storage solutions. Fiber Channel operates at different speeds, ranging from 1Gbps to 128Gbps, depending on the version of the technology being used, and is designed to provide reliable and fast data transmission in both small and large environments.

Fiber Channel's primary advantage is its ability to provide low-latency, high-bandwidth communication between servers and storage devices. This makes it an ideal solution for applications that require fast access to large amounts of data, such as databases, virtualized environments, and high-performance computing applications. Unlike Ethernet, which uses a connectionless model, Fiber Channel operates in a connection-oriented manner, ensuring that data is reliably transferred between devices. The protocol uses a lossless transmission mechanism that guarantees no data loss during the transfer process, even under heavy network load.

One of the defining features of a SAN is its ability to decouple storage resources from the individual servers that use them. In a typical server-storage configuration, each server is connected to its own dedicated storage device, which can lead to inefficiencies in resource utilization. In a SAN environment, however, multiple servers can share access to centralized storage, enabling more efficient use of storage resources. The SAN architecture allows for the consolidation of storage resources into a single pool, which can be managed and allocated as needed by various servers or applications. This centralization of storage simplifies management and improves scalability, as new storage devices can be added to the network without the need for additional direct connections to individual servers.

A SAN typically consists of several key components, including storage devices, servers, switches, and the Fiber Channel network itself. The storage devices in a SAN can include disk arrays, tape libraries, and other types of storage systems. These devices are connected to the SAN via Fiber Channel switches, which act as intermediaries, directing traffic between servers and storage devices. The switches in a SAN are essential for ensuring that data is transmitted efficiently and reliably across the network. They provide the necessary infrastructure to manage the flow of data between devices, enabling high-speed communication and low-latency access to storage.

Fiber Channel switches form the backbone of the SAN, creating a fabric that connects the various devices in the network. The switches use a routing protocol to ensure that data is directed to the appropriate destination, whether that is a server requesting data from a storage device or a storage device delivering data to a server. The fabric architecture allows for flexible and scalable network designs, as new devices can be added to the network without disrupting the existing infrastructure. The scalability of a SAN is one of its key advantages, as it can easily grow with the needs of the business, accommodating new storage devices, servers, and users as necessary.

In addition to the physical hardware, a SAN also relies on specialized management software to control and monitor the network. This software provides administrators with the tools they need to configure, manage, and troubleshoot the SAN infrastructure. The management software typically includes features such as device discovery, zoning, performance monitoring, and fault detection. Zoning is a critical function in SAN management, as it allows administrators to define which devices can communicate with each other. By grouping devices into zones, the network can be segmented into logical domains, providing better security, performance, and fault isolation.

The benefits of SAN networks are numerous, particularly for businesses that need to manage large volumes of data. SANs offer high performance, scalability, and reliability, which makes them ideal for enterprise environments that require fast and efficient access to storage resources. With SANs, businesses can centralize their storage resources, reducing the complexity of managing individual storage devices connected directly to servers. SANs also provide redundancy and fault tolerance, ensuring that data is always available, even in the event of hardware failures. This level of reliability is essential for mission-critical applications that cannot afford downtime or data loss.

In the modern era of data-driven business, the need for efficient and scalable storage solutions has never been greater. The increasing adoption of cloud computing, big data analytics, and virtualization has placed greater demands on storage systems, making it essential for businesses to invest in technologies like Fiber Channel and SANs. These technologies provide the necessary infrastructure to meet the growing demands for data storage, ensuring that businesses can store, access, and manage their data efficiently and securely.

Fiber Channel and SAN networks are not just about transferring data; they are also about ensuring that data is always available when needed, no matter the scale or complexity of the environment. By providing high-speed, low-latency access to centralized storage, Fiber Channel and SAN technologies enable businesses to maximize the value of their data while minimizing the risk of downtime or data loss. Whether for a small business or a large enterprise, the implementation of Fiber Channel and SAN networks is a crucial step in building a robust, efficient, and reliable data infrastructure.

# Understanding the Basics of Fiber Channel Technology

Fiber Channel (FC) technology is a high-speed networking protocol designed primarily for storage area networks (SANs). It provides a reliable and efficient way to transfer large amounts of data between computers and storage devices. Originally developed in the late 1980s, Fiber Channel was created to address the limitations of earlier network technologies, such as Ethernet and SCSI, particularly in the areas of speed, reliability, and scalability. Its robust design has made it a fundamental component in modern data centers, where it serves as the backbone for connecting servers, storage devices, and switches.

At its core, Fiber Channel is a data transfer protocol that operates over both copper and optical fiber cables. The technology can deliver high-speed data transmission rates ranging from 1 Gbps to as high as 128 Gbps, depending on the version of Fiber Channel used. This makes it ideal for environments where large amounts of data need to be transferred quickly and reliably, such as enterprise data centers, where both high performance and low latency are essential. The primary advantage of Fiber Channel over other networking technologies is its ability to provide a lossless and deterministic transmission of data, ensuring that all data is reliably transmitted without any loss or corruption, even under heavy traffic loads.

One of the key aspects of Fiber Channel technology is its connection-oriented nature. Unlike Ethernet, which uses a connectionless approach to transmit data, Fiber Channel establishes a dedicated communication path between devices before data transmission occurs. This approach reduces the likelihood of network congestion and ensures that data is sent efficiently, with minimal delays. Fiber Channel also supports the concept of flow control, meaning that it can manage the rate at which data is sent, preventing congestion and packet loss in the network. This is particularly important in high-demand environments where the need for uninterrupted data flow is critical.

Fiber Channel operates in a layered architecture, with each layer serving a specific function in the data transmission process. The protocol is designed to be agnostic to the type of data being transmitted, meaning that it can be used for various types of storage traffic, including block-level storage, file-level storage, and tape libraries. The upper layers of the Fiber Channel protocol define how data is formatted and transmitted, while the lower layers manage the physical and link-level aspects of the communication. This separation of layers allows Fiber Channel to maintain flexibility and scalability, as different types of devices and storage systems can be integrated into the network without affecting the performance or reliability of the overall system.

One of the defining features of Fiber Channel is its use of a switch-based fabric for routing data between devices. This fabric-based design enables the creation of highly scalable and redundant networks. Fiber Channel networks are typically organized into "zones," which define groups of devices that are allowed to communicate with each other. Zoning can be configured in various ways to control access between devices, providing enhanced security and reducing the risk of interference between devices. By using a switched fabric, Fiber Channel can scale to accommodate large numbers of devices, as new devices can be added to the network without affecting the performance of existing devices.

Another important feature of Fiber Channel technology is its support for multiple types of topologies. The most common topologies used in Fiber Channel networks are point-to-point, arbitrated loop, and switched fabric. In a point-to-point topology, two devices are directly connected, allowing for high-speed communication between them. This is a simple and efficient setup for small-scale environments but lacks scalability and flexibility. The arbitrated loop topology allows multiple devices to be connected in a loop, with each device taking turns transmitting data. While this topology is more scalable than point-to-point, it can become a bottleneck as the number of devices increases, since all devices share the same communication path. The switched fabric topology, however, offers the most scalability and flexibility, as it connects devices through a network of switches, allowing for simultaneous data transfers and the ability to add more devices without impacting overall performance.

Fiber Channel also supports several advanced features that enhance its performance and reliability. One such feature is the ability to aggregate multiple links to increase bandwidth. This is known as link aggregation or trunking, and it allows multiple Fiber Channel links to be combined into a single logical connection. By aggregating links, Fiber Channel can deliver higher data throughput and better fault tolerance, as the network can continue to operate even if one or more individual links fail. Another important feature of Fiber Channel is its support for multipathing, which enables multiple physical paths between devices. Multipathing provides redundancy, ensuring that if one path fails, the data can still be transmitted over an alternative path, minimizing downtime and improving the overall reliability of the network.

In addition to its advanced features, Fiber Channel technology is also highly secure. It uses a set of protocols and techniques to ensure that data is transmitted securely between devices. One of the key security features of Fiber Channel is its use of the Fibre Channel Security Protocol (FC-SP), which provides authentication, encryption, and data integrity. FC-SP ensures that only authorized devices can access the network, and it protects data in transit from unauthorized access or tampering. This is especially important in environments where sensitive data is being transferred, such as financial institutions or healthcare organizations.

The wide adoption of Fiber Channel in enterprise environments can be attributed to its reliability, performance, and ability to scale to meet the growing demands of modern data centers. Fiber Channel enables the consolidation of storage resources, providing businesses with the ability to centralize their storage infrastructure while ensuring fast, reliable access to data. It also supports virtualization, allowing businesses to run multiple virtual machines on a single physical server while providing each virtual machine with its own dedicated storage resources. This makes Fiber Channel an essential component in the deployment of virtualized environments, where the efficient management of storage resources is crucial.

In summary, Fiber Channel technology is a high-performance, reliable, and secure networking protocol that has become a fundamental component of storage area networks. Its ability to deliver high-speed, low-latency data transmission, coupled with its advanced features such as zoning, link aggregation, and multipathing, makes it an ideal solution for enterprises with demanding storage requirements. The flexibility and scalability of Fiber Channel allow businesses to build storage networks that can grow with their needs, ensuring that they can continue to meet the increasing demands for data storage and access. As data continues to play a central role in modern business operations, Fiber Channel technology will remain a critical enabler of high-performance, reliable, and scalable storage solutions.

# Key Components of Fiber Channel Networks

Fiber Channel networks are essential for building high-performance and scalable storage solutions in enterprise environments. To fully understand how Fiber Channel networks operate, it is important to examine the key components that make up these systems. The main components of Fiber Channel networks include the storage devices, host bus adapters (HBAs), Fiber Channel switches, and cables, all of which work together to create a robust and efficient storage infrastructure. Each component plays a specific role in ensuring that data is transferred reliably, efficiently, and securely across the network, enabling businesses to manage their data storage needs effectively.

At the heart of any Fiber Channel network is the storage device, which can take various forms such as disk arrays, tape libraries, or optical storage systems. These devices are the primary source of data storage in a Fiber Channel network and are typically designed to offer high capacity, performance, and redundancy. Storage devices in a Fiber Channel network are connected to the network through Fiber Channel host bus adapters (HBAs) or Fiber Channel over Ethernet (FCoE) adapters. These adapters allow the storage devices to communicate with other devices in the network, facilitating data transfer between servers, storage systems, and other networked devices. The storage devices can be physical or virtual, depending on the needs of the organization, and are often managed through centralized storage management systems to ensure that they provide the necessary performance and availability.

Host Bus Adapters (HBAs) are a critical component in the Fiber Channel network. An HBA is a hardware interface card that is installed in a server or computer to enable it to communicate with the Fiber Channel network. The HBA serves as the connection point between the server and the networked storage devices, facilitating the transfer of data between the server's processing unit and the storage system. HBAs are available in various speeds, ranging from 1 Gbps to 128 Gbps, depending on the version of Fiber Channel being used. The role of the HBA is to convert the server's internal data into a format that is compatible with the Fiber Channel protocol, allowing the server to access data stored on remote devices over the network. HBAs are designed to provide high throughput and low latency, ensuring that data is transferred quickly and efficiently, which is crucial for mission-critical applications and databases.

Fiber Channel switches are another essential component of Fiber Channel networks. These switches act as intermediaries that route data between devices in the network, including servers, storage devices, and other network components. Switches provide the necessary fabric to connect multiple devices in the network, allowing them to communicate with each other at high speeds. Fiber Channel switches are designed to be highly scalable, with the ability to accommodate thousands of devices within a single network. This scalability is important for growing organizations that need to expand their storage infrastructure over time. Fiber Channel switches come in various configurations, ranging from small, single-switch systems to large, multi-switch fabrics that can support complex network topologies.

The Fiber Channel switch fabric is the backbone of the network, enabling the communication between devices in a non-blocking, low-latency environment. The fabric is responsible for directing data traffic between devices, ensuring that the data reaches its destination quickly and reliably. Fiber Channel switches use a specialized protocol to manage the flow of data between devices, and they are typically designed to operate in a lossless manner, ensuring that no data is lost during transmission. The use of a switch fabric enables the network to handle multiple simultaneous connections, providing the high availability and fault tolerance required in modern data centers. In larger Fiber Channel networks, multiple switches are interconnected to form a larger fabric, allowing for even greater scalability and redundancy.

Cabling is another critical component in the design of a Fiber Channel network. Fiber Channel supports both copper and optical fiber cabling, depending on the distance and speed requirements of the network. Fiber optic cables are commonly used in high-performance environments because they can transmit data over long distances without degradation of signal quality. These cables are typically used to connect the Fiber Channel switches to storage devices, as well as to link different switches within the network fabric. Copper cables, on the other hand, are more commonly used for shorter distances or for lower-speed applications. The choice of cabling depends on the specific needs of the network, such as the distance between devices, the required data transfer speed, and the cost considerations.

The architecture of Fiber Channel networks also includes the concept of zones, which are used to group devices together based on their communication needs. Zoning is an important feature in Fiber Channel networks as it helps manage access control and security within the network. Devices in a Fiber Channel network can be divided into logical groups called zones, and these zones can be configured to limit which devices can communicate with each other. Zoning can be implemented at various levels, including port-based zoning, which restricts communication based on physical ports on the switches, and WWN (World Wide Name) zoning, which uses unique identifiers assigned to each device to define the communication paths. Zoning helps prevent unauthorized access and ensures that devices are only able to communicate with the devices they are authorized to interact with.

Fiber Channel networks also support a range of management tools that allow administrators to monitor and optimize the performance of the network. These management tools provide a centralized platform for configuring devices, monitoring traffic, diagnosing issues, and troubleshooting network problems. Network administrators can use these tools to set up and manage zoning, monitor bandwidth utilization, and track the health of devices within the network. Performance monitoring is a critical part of managing a Fiber Channel network, as it helps identify potential bottlenecks or performance issues that may arise as the network grows or as traffic patterns change over time.

The Fiber Channel protocol is designed to ensure that data is transmitted with minimal latency and maximum reliability. Fiber Channel networks achieve this through the use of advanced techniques such as flow control and congestion management. Flow control ensures that devices do not become overwhelmed with data, while congestion management techniques help optimize data transmission across the network. These features are particularly important in high-performance environments where consistent data transfer speeds are crucial for maintaining the performance of applications and databases.

As businesses continue to generate and store more data, the need for high-performance storage solutions becomes increasingly important. Fiber Channel networks provide a scalable, reliable, and high-performance solution for managing large volumes of data. By understanding the key components that make up a Fiber Channel network—storage devices, HBAs, switches, cabling, and management tools—organizations can design and deploy a storage infrastructure that meets their current and future needs. With the ability to deliver high-speed data transfer, low latency, and fault tolerance, Fiber Channel networks are well-suited to support the growing demands of modern data centers and enterprise storage environments.

# Fiber Channel Architecture and Topologies

The architecture and topologies of Fiber Channel networks are fundamental to understanding how data is transferred efficiently and reliably between servers, storage devices, and other networked systems. Fiber Channel is a high-performance protocol used primarily in storage area networks (SANs), where its low-latency, high-throughput capabilities allow businesses to manage large volumes of data with minimal disruption. The design of a Fiber Channel network ensures that data flows smoothly, efficiently, and securely between devices, meeting the high demands of enterprise environments. This chapter explores the architecture of Fiber Channel networks, focusing on the core components, and examines the different topologies used to structure these networks for various performance and scalability needs.

Fiber Channel's architecture is based on a switched fabric design that allows devices to communicate with one another using a network of switches. This architecture is highly scalable, allowing organizations to expand their network without disrupting existing connections. Fiber Channel's primary purpose is to provide high-speed, reliable communication between storage devices and servers. The network is composed of several key components: the storage devices, servers, switches, and the cabling that interconnects them. At the heart of the system is the switch fabric, which acts as the backbone of the network. It directs traffic between devices, ensuring that data reaches its destination quickly and efficiently. The switches form the connections that allow data to flow across the network and ensure that each device communicates with the right destination.

Fiber Channel operates over two main types of media: optical fiber and copper cabling. Optical fiber is preferred in large-scale installations due to its ability to carry data over long distances without degradation of signal quality. Copper cables, on the other hand, are used in shorter-distance connections and are generally more cost-effective for smaller installations. The use of fiber optics enables high data transfer rates, which are critical in high-performance environments like large data centers where large amounts of data need to be transferred rapidly and without interruption.

One of the core features of Fiber Channel is its use of different topologies to organize the network. A topology refers to the way in which devices are connected and communicate within the network. The three most common Fiber Channel topologies are point-to-point, arbitrated loop, and switched fabric. Each of these topologies has its own advantages and is suited to different types of environments.

In a point-to-point topology, two devices are directly connected to each other, creating a dedicated communication link. This topology is the simplest and most straightforward, with no intermediate devices such as switches involved. It provides a direct path for data to flow between devices, ensuring low-latency communication. Point-to-point connections are most commonly used in smaller-scale environments or where only a few devices need to communicate with each other. However, the point-to-point topology has limitations in terms of scalability and flexibility. As the number of devices grows, this topology becomes increasingly inefficient, as each device needs to be directly connected to every other device in the network.

The arbitrated loop topology is an improvement over point-to-point by allowing multiple devices to share a single communication path. In this topology, the devices are connected in a loop, and each device takes turns transmitting data over the shared link. The arbitrated loop is more scalable than the point-to-point topology, as it can support more devices using a single connection. However, as more devices are added, the performance of the network may decrease due to the shared nature of the communication path. This is because devices must wait their turn to transmit, and network congestion can result in delays.

The switched fabric topology is the most scalable and flexible of the three and is commonly used in large-scale Fiber Channel networks. In this topology, multiple devices are connected to a network of Fiber Channel switches, which route data between devices. Each device in the network communicates with the switch, which acts as an intermediary to forward data to its destination. The switch fabric enables multiple devices to communicate simultaneously, as the switches use an efficient routing protocol to ensure that data is directed to the correct device. This topology provides high scalability, as new devices can be added to the network without affecting the performance of existing devices. It also ensures high availability and fault tolerance, as the network can be designed with redundant switches and links to prevent a single point of failure.

Fiber Channel networks that use a switched fabric topology are organized into a network fabric, where multiple switches are interconnected to form a larger, more complex network. The fabric allows for a flexible, scalable network that can support a growing number of devices without compromising performance. The switches in the fabric communicate with each other to maintain the integrity of the network and ensure that data is transmitted efficiently. The use of multiple switches allows for redundancy, so if one switch fails, the network can continue to operate by rerouting traffic through alternate paths.

One of the most important advantages of the switched fabric topology is its ability to support zoning, a method used to control which devices can communicate with each other. Zoning is implemented at the switch level, and it allows administrators to define groups of devices that are allowed to communicate within the network. By creating separate zones, administrators can ensure that sensitive data is isolated from other parts of the network, improving security and performance. Zoning also helps manage network traffic and reduce congestion by limiting the number of devices that can access specific resources at any given time.

In addition to the basic topologies, Fiber Channel networks support several advanced features that enhance performance, reliability, and scalability. These include link aggregation, which combines multiple physical links into a single logical connection to increase bandwidth, and multipathing, which allows for multiple data paths between devices to provide redundancy and load balancing. These features are particularly useful in large-scale networks where high availability and fault tolerance are critical.

Fiber Channel networks can be further optimized by using techniques such as Quality of Service (QoS) and traffic prioritization. QoS ensures that critical applications or services receive higher priority in terms of bandwidth allocation, reducing the risk of congestion or delays for mission-critical data. Traffic prioritization ensures that high-priority data is transmitted first, ensuring that performance remains optimal even during periods of heavy network traffic.

Fiber Channel networks are also designed to support long-distance data transmission, making them suitable for geographically dispersed environments. With the use of Fiber Channel over IP (FCIP), Fiber Channel can be extended across wide-area networks (WANs), allowing organizations to connect remote data centers and storage facilities. This enables businesses to implement disaster recovery solutions by replicating data between locations to ensure business continuity in the event of a failure.

Fiber Channel architecture and topologies are fundamental to understanding how large-scale storage systems are designed and implemented. The scalability, flexibility, and reliability of Fiber Channel networks make them the ideal choice for organizations that need to manage vast amounts of data efficiently. Whether using point-to-point, arbitrated loop, or switched fabric topologies, Fiber Channel offers a high-performance solution that can meet the demands of modern data centers and enterprise storage environments. The use of advanced features such as zoning, multipathing, and QoS further enhances the ability of Fiber Channel to provide secure, reliable, and high-speed data transmission in complex storage networks.

# SAN Overview: Definition and Key Concepts

A Storage Area Network (SAN) is a high-performance, dedicated network that provides centralized storage and enables fast and reliable data access for servers and other networked devices. SANs are primarily used in enterprise environments where large volumes of data need to be stored and accessed quickly and efficiently. Unlike traditional direct-attached storage (DAS), where storage devices are directly connected to individual servers, SANs offer a more flexible and scalable solution by separating storage from the server infrastructure and allowing multiple servers to access the same storage resources over a network. The use of SAN technology significantly improves storage utilization, scalability, and performance, making it an essential component in modern data centers and businesses with large storage needs.

The key concept behind SAN is the decoupling of storage from individual servers. In traditional storage configurations, each server is connected to its own dedicated storage device, often resulting in inefficiency and underutilization of storage resources. SANs eliminate this limitation by providing a shared pool of storage that can be accessed by multiple servers simultaneously. This centralized approach allows for better resource management, as storage can be allocated dynamically based on the needs of the system or specific applications. By consolidating storage into a single network, businesses can improve storage efficiency, reduce hardware costs, and simplify management tasks.

At its core, a SAN is a specialized network designed specifically for high-speed data transfer between servers and storage devices. The most common protocol used in SANs is Fiber Channel, which provides the necessary performance, reliability, and scalability to support large-scale data environments. Fiber Channel networks are typically built using switches, host bus adapters (HBAs), and cables that allow devices to communicate with each other at high speeds. Fiber Channel provides low-latency, high-bandwidth communication, ensuring that data can be accessed quickly and efficiently by servers and other devices within the network. Additionally, Fiber Channel is designed to operate with minimal packet loss, which is crucial for maintaining data integrity in enterprise environments where data is critical.

SANs can also be built using other protocols such as iSCSI and Fibre Channel over Ethernet (FCoE). While Fiber Channel remains the most widely used protocol in SANs, iSCSI is becoming increasingly popular due to its lower cost and ease of deployment. iSCSI uses standard Ethernet infrastructure, which reduces the need for specialized hardware and cabling. FCoE, on the other hand, combines the benefits of Fiber Channel and Ethernet by enabling Fiber Channel traffic to be transmitted over Ethernet networks. Each of these protocols has its own advantages and is selected based on factors such as cost, performance requirements, and existing network infrastructure.

A key concept within SANs is the switch fabric. A switch fabric is a network of Fiber Channel switches that connect all devices within the SAN, including servers and storage devices. The switch fabric is responsible for directing data traffic between devices, ensuring that data is transmitted to the correct destination without delay or interference. This fabric-based approach allows for a highly scalable and flexible network, as new devices can be added to the SAN without disrupting existing operations. The fabric enables multiple devices to communicate simultaneously, improving overall network efficiency and ensuring that data can be accessed without bottlenecks.

Another important concept in SANs is zoning, which provides a mechanism for controlling access to storage devices and improving security. Zoning allows administrators to group devices into logical zones, where only the devices within a specific zone can communicate with each other. This segmentation helps reduce the risk of unauthorized access and ensures that devices only have access to the resources they need. Zoning can be configured based on different criteria, such as device type, function, or location. This flexibility makes zoning an important tool for managing large and complex SANs, where security and access control are critical.

In a SAN environment, multipathing is another important concept that improves the reliability and performance of the network. Multipathing allows for multiple physical paths to be established between servers and storage devices, ensuring that if one path fails, data can still be transmitted over an alternate path. This redundancy increases the fault tolerance of the SAN, reducing the risk of downtime due to network failures. Multipathing also helps optimize performance by distributing data traffic across multiple paths, preventing any single path from becoming overloaded. This ensures that data can be accessed quickly and efficiently, even in high-demand environments.

SANs are typically managed through specialized software that provides administrators with the tools needed to configure, monitor, and troubleshoot the network. SAN management software enables administrators to manage storage resources, monitor performance, and perform tasks such as backup and disaster recovery. The software also provides tools for provisioning storage, which allows administrators to allocate storage resources to servers and applications as needed. The ability to dynamically allocate storage resources based on demand is one of the key benefits of SANs, as it allows businesses to respond quickly to changing storage needs without the need for manual intervention.

The scalability of SANs is one of their most important features. As businesses grow and storage requirements increase, SANs can be easily expanded to accommodate more devices and higher data volumes. The use of a switch fabric ensures that new devices can be added to the network without disrupting existing operations, making SANs highly adaptable to changing business needs. Furthermore, SANs can be used to connect storage devices across multiple geographic locations, enabling businesses to implement disaster recovery solutions and ensure business continuity in the event of a failure. By replicating data across multiple sites, organizations can ensure that critical data is always available, even in the event of a disaster.

One of the key advantages of SANs is their ability to improve the performance of applications and databases. By providing fast, low-latency access to storage resources, SANs enable applications to run more efficiently, with reduced wait times for data retrieval. This is particularly important in environments where large amounts of data need to be processed quickly, such as in financial services, healthcare, and e-commerce. The centralized nature of SANs also allows for better data management and data protection, as storage resources can be easily backed up, replicated, and restored.

In enterprise environments, SANs are often integrated with other technologies such as virtualization and cloud storage to further enhance their capabilities. Virtualization allows multiple virtual machines to access shared storage resources in a way that is transparent to the underlying hardware, improving resource utilization and flexibility. Cloud storage integration enables businesses to store and access data remotely, providing greater scalability and cost efficiency. By leveraging these technologies, businesses can create a more dynamic and flexible storage infrastructure that can grow with their needs.

In summary, SANs are an essential technology for businesses that require high-performance, scalable, and reliable storage solutions.

They provide centralized storage that can be accessed by multiple servers and applications, improving efficiency and reducing hardware costs. By utilizing protocols such as Fiber Channel, iSCSI, and FCoE, SANs offer the performance and reliability needed to support modern enterprise applications. The key concepts of switch fabrics, zoning, multipathing, and dynamic provisioning ensure that SANs can be tailored to meet the specific needs of an organization, providing a flexible and secure storage solution.

# Fiber Channel vs. iSCSI: A Comparative Analysis

In the realm of modern data storage, two dominant technologies for implementing Storage Area Networks (SANs) are Fiber Channel (FC) and Internet Small Computer Systems Interface (iSCSI). Both technologies enable high-speed data transfer between servers and storage devices, but they do so using different methods, protocols, and hardware requirements. While both solutions offer distinct advantages, their key differences lie in performance, cost, scalability, and network infrastructure compatibility. Understanding these differences is essential for organizations looking to select the right technology for their specific needs, particularly when considering the unique requirements of storage-intensive environments such as data centers or virtualized infrastructures.

Fiber Channel, developed in the late 1980s, is a high-speed network protocol specifically designed for storage networks. It operates over a dedicated network and provides a robust, low-latency method for transmitting data between servers and storage devices. Fiber Channel networks are typically based on fiber optic cables, although copper can also be used in shorter-range configurations. The protocol itself offers exceptionally high throughput, with speeds ranging from 1 Gbps to 128 Gbps in its latest iterations. Fiber Channel is renowned for its ability to provide high reliability, scalability, and low-latency communication, which is crucial in environments where performance and uptime are critical, such as in enterprise data centers.

iSCSI, on the other hand, is a more recent protocol that operates over standard Ethernet networks, enabling the use of existing network infrastructure for storage communication. iSCSI works by encapsulating SCSI commands, which are used for reading and writing data from storage devices, into IP packets. These packets are then transmitted over TCP/IP networks. The widespread use of Ethernet makes iSCSI an attractive solution for businesses already operating in environments where Ethernet is the primary network communication medium. iSCSI operates over much more cost-effective hardware, with no need for specialized switches or cabling, which makes it an appealing choice for smaller organizations or those with less demanding storage needs.

The fundamental difference between Fiber Channel and iSCSI lies in their respective network architectures. Fiber Channel typically operates over a dedicated network called a SAN fabric, which requires specialized Fiber Channel switches and HBAs (Host Bus Adapters) installed in servers. This dedicated network provides the high performance, redundancy, and fault tolerance that enterprises demand. By isolating storage traffic from general network traffic, Fiber Channel ensures that data is transmitted with minimal delay and maximum throughput, even during periods of heavy usage.

iSCSI, in contrast, leverages existing Ethernet networks, making it more versatile in terms of hardware requirements. Ethernet is already prevalent in most organizations, so adopting iSCSI typically requires minimal additional investment in infrastructure. iSCSI allows organizations to utilize standard Ethernet switches, network cards, and cabling, which significantly reduces both initial setup costs and operational expenses. While iSCSI can operate at high speeds, its performance is largely dependent on the underlying Ethernet infrastructure. As Ethernet networks are often shared between multiple applications and users, the potential for network congestion or performance degradation is higher compared to the dedicated Fiber Channel network.

In terms of performance, Fiber Channel has the edge in environments where high throughput and low latency are paramount. Its design is optimized for data transfer speed, and its dedicated network ensures that storage traffic does not compete with general network traffic, making it highly predictable and reliable. Fiber Channel's protocol and hardware are designed to handle large amounts of data with minimal packet loss, making it the preferred choice for mission-critical applications like databases, virtualized environments, and high-performance computing (HPC). Its advanced features, such as link aggregation and multipathing, further enhance its ability to manage large volumes of data efficiently and provide redundancy.

While iSCSI can offer impressive speeds, particularly with 10GbE and 40GbE Ethernet connections, it is typically not as fast as Fiber Channel, especially when handling large datasets or performing high-throughput operations. The performance of iSCSI can be affected by network congestion, as Ethernet is often used for multiple types of data traffic, including non-storage-related communications. Although iSCSI has evolved to support higher speeds, its performance is more variable and may not meet the stringent requirements of high-performance environments without significant network optimizations and dedicated infrastructure.

Cost is another critical factor when comparing Fiber Channel and iSCSI. Fiber Channel requires specialized hardware, including Fiber Channel switches, cables, and HBAs, all of which can be expensive. This makes Fiber Channel a more costly solution, particularly for small and medium-sized enterprises that may not require the level of performance and scalability offered by this technology. Additionally, Fiber Channel networks often require more complex management and troubleshooting, which can further increase operational costs.

iSCSI, on the other hand, is considerably less expensive to implement because it uses standard Ethernet infrastructure. Many businesses already have Ethernet-based networks in place, and they can often leverage existing hardware like Ethernet switches and network interface cards (NICs) to deploy iSCSI. This makes iSCSI a more affordable option, particularly for smaller organizations or those with limited budgets for storage networking. The lower cost of iSCSI does not necessarily mean it sacrifices flexibility or performance for certain use cases. For many applications, particularly those that do not require ultra-high performance, iSCSI provides an effective and cost-efficient solution.

In terms of scalability, both Fiber Channel and iSCSI are capable of handling large storage environments, but the ease with which they scale differs. Fiber Channel networks are highly scalable, and as an enterprise grows, additional switches, HBAs, and storage devices can be added to the network to accommodate the increased demand. Fiber Channel also supports complex configurations, such as zoning, which allows for efficient management of large-scale environments. The use of switch fabrics further enhances the scalability and redundancy of the network.

iSCSI is also scalable, but the scalability is more directly tied to the capacity and performance of the underlying Ethernet network. Expanding an iSCSI network often requires ensuring that the Ethernet infrastructure is capable of handling increased bandwidth, which may necessitate upgrading switches, cabling, and other network components. While iSCSI networks are easier to expand in terms of cost and infrastructure, they may face limitations as the demand for storage increases, particularly if the Ethernet network is already heavily used by other applications.

Security is another consideration when comparing the two technologies. Fiber Channel networks are often considered more secure than iSCSI because they operate on a dedicated network, minimizing the risk of exposure to other types of data traffic. Fiber Channel also offers built-in features like zoning and access control, which help secure the network and control which devices can communicate with each other. iSCSI, on the other hand, operates over TCP/IP, which is inherently more vulnerable to security threats. However, iSCSI can still be secured using methods like IPsec encryption and VLANs, though this requires additional configuration and management.

Both Fiber Channel and iSCSI have their strengths and weaknesses, making them suitable for different types of environments. Fiber Channel excels in high-performance, high-availability scenarios where throughput and low latency are critical, while iSCSI offers a more cost-effective and flexible solution that can be implemented over existing Ethernet networks. The decision between the two depends on factors such as performance requirements, budget, existing infrastructure, and scalability needs. Ultimately, understanding the unique strengths of both technologies helps businesses make an informed decision about which protocol is best suited to their storage environment.

# The Role of Switches in Fiber Channel Networks

In any Fiber Channel (FC) network, switches play an essential and central role. They serve as the critical infrastructure that interconnects the various devices within the network, facilitating the seamless transfer of data between servers, storage devices, and other networked components. Fiber Channel, a high-performance protocol primarily used in Storage Area Networks (SANs), relies heavily on switches to enable high-speed, reliable communication across potentially vast and complex networks. Without switches, a Fiber Channel network would struggle to achieve the level of performance, scalability, and fault tolerance that it is known for. Understanding the function of switches in Fiber Channel networks helps clarify how they contribute to the overall efficiency and reliability of storage environments, especially in large-scale data centers and enterprise storage solutions.

At the core of a Fiber Channel network, switches perform the task of routing data between devices, such as servers and storage arrays. Fiber Channel operates as a dedicated, high-speed, low-latency network specifically designed for storage traffic, making the need for high-performance switches critical. The switches are responsible for determining the optimal path for data packets to travel across the network, ensuring that information is directed to the appropriate destination in the most efficient manner possible. They manage and direct traffic to ensure that the network remains efficient even as it scales, providing the necessary infrastructure to handle high volumes of data traffic without congestion or delay.

Fiber Channel switches enable devices to communicate within a "fabric," which is a network architecture that connects multiple devices in a way that allows them to exchange data without direct connections to each other. The fabric created by the switches forms the backbone of the network, enabling the creation of large, distributed, and highly available storage environments. The use of a switched fabric, where each device is connected through a network of switches, makes Fiber Channel inherently more flexible and scalable compared to direct-attached storage (DAS) or other networking protocols. As new devices are added to the network, the fabric automatically accommodates them without disrupting the performance or operation of existing devices.

One of the key functions of switches in a Fiber Channel network is the management of data paths. These switches use routing algorithms to determine the best way for data to travel from one device to another. By connecting all devices in the network through a fabric of switches, Fiber Channel ensures that data can travel across multiple possible paths, increasing redundancy and reliability. In cases of a link failure or congestion, the switches can automatically reroute data through alternate paths, ensuring that communication remains uninterrupted. This level of fault tolerance is critical in mission-critical environments where downtime can lead to significant operational disruptions.

Another important feature of Fiber Channel switches is their ability to support zoning. Zoning is a method used to control access between devices in the network, essentially partitioning the fabric into isolated regions. By creating zones, administrators can ensure that only authorized devices are allowed to communicate with each other, improving security and reducing the risk of unauthorized access. Zoning is particularly important in environments where sensitive or critical data is stored, as it helps prevent unauthorized devices from accessing particular resources. This segmentation of the network enhances both performance and security by limiting the scope of device interactions, ensuring that traffic remains confined within designated areas.

Fiber Channel switches also provide the ability to implement virtual fabrics, which allow for even further logical segmentation of the network. A virtual fabric is essentially a subset of a larger Fiber Channel fabric that can be managed independently. This enables organizations to create multiple isolated networks within the same physical infrastructure, improving both management efficiency and security. Virtual fabrics are particularly useful in multi-tenant environments, where different departments or applications require isolated storage resources but still need to operate within the same physical network.

In addition to managing traffic flow and enabling zoning, switches are crucial for ensuring that data is transferred at the highest possible speeds with minimal latency. Fiber Channel switches are designed to operate in a lossless mode, which means that they guarantee that data will be delivered accurately without any loss during transmission. This is crucial in environments where data integrity is paramount, such as databases or financial systems, where even a small loss of data can have severe consequences. The lossless nature of Fiber Channel also allows for more predictable and stable performance, as devices do not need to retransmit lost packets, which could otherwise slow down the network.

Fiber Channel switches come in different configurations to accommodate the varying needs of organizations. In smaller, simpler networks, a single switch might be sufficient to connect a few devices, but as the network grows, the complexity increases. Larger organizations may deploy multi-switch fabrics that are interconnected to form a more complex and highly scalable network. These switches work together to handle greater volumes of data traffic, distribute load, and provide redundancy. The architecture of these multi-switch fabrics is designed to ensure that there are no single points of failure, making the network highly resilient. In the event that one switch fails, the traffic is automatically rerouted through other available switches, ensuring continued operation without disruption.

The performance of Fiber Channel networks, especially in large environments, also depends on the proper management and optimization of the switches. Network administrators use management software to configure switches, monitor traffic, diagnose issues, and make necessary adjustments to optimize performance. These management tools allow administrators to track network health, monitor traffic patterns, and identify potential bottlenecks. In environments where performance is critical, such as in virtualized systems or high-performance computing (HPC) setups, managing the flow of data through the switches is essential for maintaining overall system efficiency.

Additionally, Fiber Channel switches enable advanced features such as Quality of Service (QoS) and traffic prioritization. QoS mechanisms ensure that high-priority data, such as real-time transactions or mission-critical applications, are given precedence over less critical traffic. This ensures that bandwidth is allocated efficiently, and the most important data gets through even when the network is under heavy load. Traffic prioritization helps maintain predictable performance in environments with high data throughput demands, ensuring that critical applications are not delayed by other network traffic.

The role of Fiber Channel switches in modern data centers is indispensable, as they form the backbone of the storage infrastructure. They enable high-speed, low-latency data transmission, provide fault tolerance, and help ensure that data is always available when needed. Through their ability to create scalable, resilient networks, switches allow organizations to expand their storage systems without compromising performance or reliability. Whether used in small-scale environments or large, distributed SANs, Fiber Channel switches provide the foundation for high-performance storage solutions that meet the demanding needs of today's enterprise applications. As data continues to grow in volume and complexity, the role of switches in Fiber Channel networks will remain integral to ensuring that storage systems remain fast, reliable, and scalable.

# Understanding SAN Switch Fabric Design

Storage Area Networks (SANs) have become a crucial part of modern data center infrastructure, providing high-speed and reliable data storage solutions for businesses. The design of a SAN switch fabric is an essential aspect of ensuring the performance, scalability, and reliability of these networks. A SAN switch fabric is a network of interconnected Fiber Channel switches that forms the backbone of a SAN, enabling the efficient transfer of data between servers, storage devices, and other networked components. Understanding the design and operation of SAN switch fabrics is fundamental for administrators and engineers who aim to build and maintain highly performant and scalable storage solutions.

At its core, a SAN switch fabric is a collection of switches connected in a way that allows for efficient and redundant data transfer between devices within the SAN. The switch fabric acts as the central communication hub, connecting servers, storage devices, and other components in a high-speed, low-latency network. This architecture allows data to flow freely between devices, ensuring that large volumes of data can be transferred quickly and reliably across the network. The fabric is designed to handle multiple simultaneous connections and data flows, ensuring that performance remains stable even under heavy load.

A key feature of SAN switch fabric design is the concept of non-blocking communication. In a non-blocking network, data can be transmitted between devices without interference or contention for bandwidth. This ensures that each device has the ability to communicate with other devices at the maximum available bandwidth, without being slowed down by other devices on the network. The non-blocking nature of SAN fabrics is achieved through the use of high-speed, low-latency switches that can direct traffic efficiently and without congestion. As the number of devices and data traffic in the network grows, the design of the switch fabric becomes increasingly important to ensure that the network remains fast and responsive.

The switch fabric plays a central role in the scalability of SANs. One of the primary advantages of a SAN switch fabric is its ability to scale as the storage and networking needs of an organization increase. As new devices are added to the network, they can be easily integrated into the fabric without disrupting the overall performance of the system. This scalability is achieved through the use of modular switches that can be expanded as needed, allowing for the seamless addition of new devices, storage arrays, and servers. The switch fabric can support thousands of devices, providing a flexible and scalable architecture that can grow with the needs of the organization.

Redundancy is another key aspect of SAN switch fabric design. To ensure high availability and fault tolerance, SAN fabrics are typically designed with multiple switches and redundant paths between devices. This redundancy ensures that the network can continue to operate even if one or more switches fail. If a switch or link becomes unavailable, the fabric automatically reroutes traffic through alternate paths, minimizing downtime and maintaining network performance. The use of redundant switches and paths provides the fault tolerance necessary for mission-critical applications and ensures that data is always accessible, even in the event of hardware failure.

One of the key design considerations in SAN switch fabrics is the use of zoning. Zoning is a method of segmenting the fabric into smaller, isolated sections that control which devices can communicate with each other. Zoning is typically implemented at the switch level and can be based on various criteria, such as the World Wide Name (WWN) of a device or the physical port on the switch. By defining zones within the fabric, administrators can create secure, isolated environments where only specific devices are allowed to communicate with one another. This enhances both security and performance by limiting unnecessary traffic between devices and reducing the potential for unauthorized access.

Zoning also helps with traffic management in larger SANs by reducing congestion and improving overall network efficiency. By limiting communication to only the devices within a particular zone, the fabric can ensure that traffic is directed only to the necessary devices, reducing the overall load on the network and improving performance. Zoning can be configured in different ways depending on the needs of the organization, with options such as hard zoning, soft zoning, and mixed zoning. Each zoning method provides a different level of control and flexibility, allowing administrators to tailor the fabric design to the specific requirements of the SAN.

Another important consideration in SAN switch fabric design is the choice of switch topology. The topology of a SAN switch fabric refers to the physical and logical arrangement of the switches and devices in the network. Common topologies include the point-to-point, arbitrated loop, and switched fabric topologies. In a point-to-point topology, devices are directly connected to one another, forming a simple and straightforward network. While this topology is easy to implement, it lacks scalability and flexibility. In an arbitrated loop topology, devices are connected in a loop, with each device taking turns to communicate. While this provides a more scalable solution than point-to-point, it can result in bottlenecks as the number of devices increases.

The switched fabric topology, which is the most commonly used in modern SANs, allows for multiple switches to be interconnected, forming a highly scalable and flexible network. The switches in a switched fabric work together to route data between devices, ensuring that data flows efficiently and reliably. The switched fabric topology is highly resilient, as it allows for multiple paths between devices, ensuring that if one path fails, data can be rerouted through an alternate path without interrupting communication. This redundancy and fault tolerance make the switched fabric topology ideal for mission-critical applications and large-scale SANs.

The design of a SAN switch fabric also requires careful consideration of the bandwidth and speed requirements of the network. Fiber Channel networks can support speeds ranging from 1 Gbps to 128 Gbps, depending on the version of the protocol and the hardware used. The bandwidth requirements of the SAN must be taken into account when designing the switch fabric, as the switches must be able to handle the volume of data traffic without creating bottlenecks or performance issues. High-speed switches with large backplane capacity are essential for ensuring that the fabric can handle the growing demands of the network.

In addition to the physical design of the switch fabric, network management and monitoring are essential to ensuring the performance and health of the SAN. Fiber Channel networks rely on management software to configure, monitor, and troubleshoot the switch fabric. These management tools provide administrators with real-time insights into the health of the fabric, including information on switch performance, link status, and traffic flow. By actively monitoring the fabric, administrators can identify potential issues before they become critical and take corrective actions to maintain optimal network performance.

The design and implementation of a SAN switch fabric are crucial to the overall success of a Storage Area Network. A well-designed fabric ensures that data can be transferred efficiently, securely, and reliably across the network, meeting the needs of the business and its applications. Scalability, redundancy, zoning, and switch topology all play important roles in the fabric's ability to provide high availability, fault tolerance, and optimal performance. By understanding the key design principles and considerations involved in building a SAN switch fabric, organizations can create a storage infrastructure that is capable of supporting their data needs both now and in the future.

# Fiber Channel Network Zoning: Concepts and Methods

Fiber Channel networks are designed to facilitate high-speed, reliable communication between storage devices and servers in a storage area network (SAN). One of the key features that enhance the efficiency, security, and scalability of Fiber Channel networks is zoning. Zoning is the process of creating logical divisions within the network, allowing administrators to control which devices can communicate with each other. This segmentation improves performance by reducing unnecessary traffic, enhances security by limiting access, and simplifies network management by creating manageable groups of devices. Understanding the concepts and methods of zoning is crucial for designing and maintaining efficient Fiber Channel networks.

The fundamental concept of zoning in Fiber Channel networks is to divide the SAN fabric into smaller, isolated zones. Each zone consists of a group of devices that can communicate with each other, but devices in different zones cannot directly communicate unless they are specifically permitted to do so. Zoning provides a way to manage access to storage resources, ensuring that only authorized devices within a specific zone can interact with particular storage devices. This segmentation reduces the risk of unauthorized access, preventing malicious or accidental interference between devices that should not be communicating with each other. Zoning also improves network efficiency by controlling the flow of data and preventing unnecessary traffic between devices that do not need to communicate.

One of the primary benefits of zoning is security. By creating zones, administrators can prevent devices from interacting with each other unless they are part of the same zone. For example, sensitive data stored on a storage device can be isolated from other devices in the network by placing it in a separate zone. This minimizes the chances of unauthorized access or data breaches. Zoning is particularly useful in environments where compliance with data security regulations is critical, such as in healthcare or financial industries, where access to sensitive data needs to be tightly controlled.

In addition to security, zoning helps manage performance. By limiting communication to devices within a specific zone, the network can reduce congestion and ensure that data is transmitted only to devices that need it. This segmentation can be particularly beneficial in large-scale SAN environments where many devices are connected. Without zoning, a single device might broadcast traffic to all other devices in the network, leading to potential bottlenecks and inefficient use of bandwidth. Zoning prevents this by ensuring that communication is only allowed between devices that are part of the same zone, optimizing the use of network resources and ensuring that traffic is directed to the appropriate destinations.

Zoning also simplifies network management by organizing devices into logical groups based on their function, location, or purpose. In a large SAN, with many storage devices and servers, managing the network can become complex. Zoning allows administrators to group devices into zones based on specific criteria, making it easier to manage and troubleshoot the network. For example, all servers in a particular department or application can be grouped into a zone, while storage devices used by those servers are placed in the same zone. This logical grouping allows for easier monitoring and management, as devices in the same zone can be treated as a single unit for configuration, troubleshooting, and monitoring purposes.

There are several methods of implementing zoning in Fiber Channel networks, each providing different levels of control and flexibility. The two most common types of zoning are port-based zoning and World Wide Name (WWN)-based zoning. Port-based zoning is the simplest and most straightforward method. In port-based zoning, the communication between devices is controlled based on the physical ports to which they are connected. Devices are placed in a zone based on the specific switch ports to which they are connected. This method is easy to configure but has limitations when it comes to flexibility and scalability. If a device is moved to a different port, it must be manually reconfigured to ensure it remains in the correct zone.

WWN-based zoning, on the other hand, provides greater flexibility and scalability. In WWN-based zoning, devices are assigned to zones based on their unique World Wide Name, which is a globally unique identifier for each Fiber Channel device. This method allows devices to maintain their membership in a zone regardless of which switch port they are connected to. WWN-based zoning is particularly useful in environments where devices are frequently moved or reconfigured, as it ensures that the zoning configuration remains intact even when devices are relocated within the network. WWN zoning is also more scalable, as it allows for more dynamic management of devices without the need to reconfigure physical ports.

In addition to port-based and WWN-based zoning, there are hybrid zoning methods that combine elements of both approaches. Hybrid zoning allows administrators to define zones based on a combination of port numbers and WWNs, providing greater flexibility and control over the network. This method is particularly useful in large, complex environments where different types of devices with varying needs are connected to the same switches. Hybrid zoning allows for more granular control over device communication, enabling administrators to create more precise and customized zoning configurations.

Zoning can also be further enhanced through the use of access control lists (ACLs), which provide additional layers of security and control. ACLs allow administrators to define specific rules that determine which devices are allowed to communicate with each other, based on factors such as IP address, protocol, or device type. ACLs are particularly useful in larger SAN environments where more detailed control over access is required. By combining zoning with ACLs, administrators can create highly secure and efficient networks that ensure only authorized devices can access specific resources.

The implementation of zoning is not without its challenges. One of the key challenges is the complexity of managing large numbers of zones in a large-scale SAN. As the number of devices and zones increases, it can become difficult to keep track of the relationships between devices and ensure that the zoning configuration remains accurate. Additionally, changes to the network, such as adding or removing devices, require careful attention to ensure that the zoning configuration is updated accordingly. Proper network documentation, regular audits, and effective monitoring tools can help mitigate these challenges by ensuring that zoning configurations are consistent and up-to-date.

Another challenge is the potential for network fragmentation. Zoning is a powerful tool for controlling access and improving performance, but it can also create isolated network segments that do not communicate with each other. This fragmentation can lead to difficulties in accessing resources across different zones and can increase the complexity of network management. However, with proper planning and management, these issues can be mitigated, and zoning can continue to provide significant benefits in terms of security, performance, and scalability.

Zoning in Fiber Channel networks is an essential tool for improving the security, performance, and manageability of SANs. By creating logical divisions within the network, administrators can control access, reduce congestion, and simplify the management of large-scale storage environments. The flexibility of zoning methods, including port-based and WWN-based zoning, allows administrators to tailor the network to meet specific needs and ensure that devices communicate efficiently. While zoning presents some challenges, its benefits far outweigh the difficulties, making it a critical component of any Fiber Channel network design.

# Fiber Channel Link Aggregation and Multipathing

Fiber Channel technology is well-regarded for its high-speed data transfer capabilities, low-latency communication, and reliability in the context of storage area networks (SANs). However, as data volumes continue to grow and the demand for uninterrupted access to storage resources becomes more critical, additional strategies must be employed to ensure that Fiber Channel networks can maintain performance, reliability, and redundancy. Two essential strategies for achieving this are link aggregation and multipathing. Both of these methods enhance network throughput and fault tolerance, enabling

Fiber Channel networks to scale effectively while minimizing the impact of potential disruptions. Understanding how these techniques work and how they can be implemented in a SAN is key to optimizing the performance and resilience of modern storage environments.

Link aggregation, also referred to as trunking or port-channeling, involves combining multiple physical links into a single logical connection to increase the overall bandwidth available between devices. This technique is widely used in network environments where high data transfer rates are crucial, and Fiber Channel is no exception. By aggregating several links, Fiber Channel can effectively multiply the available bandwidth, thus alleviating congestion and improving the overall throughput of the network. Link aggregation provides a means of increasing the capacity of the network without needing to add more physical switches or devices. Instead, administrators can simply add additional links between switches or between switches and storage devices, and the network will treat them as a single, higher-capacity logical link.

The primary advantage of link aggregation is the significant increase in bandwidth. For instance, if a network has several 16 Gbps links between switches, by aggregating them, the network can deliver 64 Gbps of combined bandwidth. This allows for more efficient data transfers and greater flexibility in managing larger data workloads. The use of multiple links for a single connection also enhances load balancing, as data traffic can be distributed across the aggregated links, optimizing the performance of the network.

In addition to increasing bandwidth, link aggregation also enhances fault tolerance and redundancy. In the event that one of the physical links in the aggregation fails, the remaining links can continue to carry traffic, ensuring that data transfer is not interrupted. This makes link aggregation an essential component for ensuring the reliability of Fiber Channel networks. For example, in large-scale SAN environments, where downtime can lead to significant business disruptions, having multiple paths for data transmission ensures that the network remains operational even in the face of hardware failures.

Multipathing, on the other hand, is a technique used to provide multiple physical paths between servers and storage devices, enhancing both redundancy and performance. Multipathing involves configuring the SAN to allow data to travel along more than one physical path simultaneously, ensuring that the network can continue to function even if one of the paths becomes unavailable. Multipathing can be implemented at the host level, storage array level, or network switch level, and it provides a high degree of fault tolerance for mission-critical applications that cannot afford to lose access to storage.

Multipathing offers several key benefits, the most significant of which is its ability to provide redundancy. By having multiple physical paths between devices, the network can continue to function seamlessly even if one path fails. This fault tolerance is vital in high-availability environments, where ensuring continuous data access is a priority. For example, if one of the fiber optic cables or switches that forms part of a path fails, the multipathing technology automatically reroutes the traffic over another available path, minimizing downtime and ensuring the integrity of the data transfer.

Another advantage of multipathing is its ability to improve load balancing and optimize performance. In a multipath setup, the data is distributed across the available paths, which prevents any single path from becoming overloaded. This ensures that the available bandwidth is used efficiently and prevents network bottlenecks. In situations where multiple servers or applications are accessing the same storage device, multipathing can help prevent congestion and ensure that all devices are able to operate at their full potential. In this way, multipathing contributes to both the performance and the reliability of Fiber Channel networks.

When configuring multipathing, administrators can select from different algorithms and policies for load balancing. These algorithms control how traffic is distributed across the available paths, and they can be adjusted to meet the specific needs of the environment. For instance, a round-robin load balancing algorithm would distribute traffic evenly across all available paths, while a weighted algorithm might prioritize certain paths based on factors such as their bandwidth or latency characteristics. The choice of load balancing algorithm is essential for optimizing the performance of the SAN, particularly in environments where high availability and performance are paramount.

Both link aggregation and multipathing work together to ensure that Fiber Channel networks can scale efficiently and maintain performance in high-demand environments. While link aggregation primarily focuses on increasing bandwidth by combining multiple physical links into a single logical link, multipathing offers redundancy by providing multiple paths between devices. The combination of these two techniques ensures that the network can handle larger data loads, maintain high availability, and continue to function even in the event of a failure.

One of the key considerations when implementing link aggregation and multipathing in a Fiber Channel network is the need for compatible hardware and software. For link aggregation, the switches, cables, and host bus adapters (HBAs) used in the network must support the necessary protocols for aggregating links. Similarly, multipathing requires the proper configuration of both the servers and the storage devices to ensure that traffic can be routed across multiple paths. Additionally, management software is often used to monitor and control the paths, ensuring that traffic is properly balanced and that any failures in the network are quickly detected and addressed.

The use of link aggregation and multipathing in Fiber Channel networks also requires careful planning and design to ensure that the network remains efficient and resilient. When aggregating links, administrators must consider the physical layout of the network, as well as the available bandwidth and potential bottlenecks. For multipathing, it is essential to ensure that there are enough available paths to support the desired level of redundancy and load balancing. Proper network monitoring tools are also needed to track the health of the paths and ensure that data is being routed efficiently and without interruption.

Link aggregation and multipathing are both essential techniques for building high-performance, fault-tolerant Fiber Channel networks. They ensure that data can be transmitted efficiently, reliably, and without interruption, even in the face of hardware failures or high traffic loads. These technologies provide scalability and flexibility, allowing organizations to meet the increasing demands of modern data storage environments. As data volumes grow and the need for continuous access to storage resources becomes more critical, the use of link aggregation and multipathing will remain central to the design and operation of robust, high-performing Fiber Channel networks.

# Fiber Channel over Ethernet (FCoE)

Fiber Channel over Ethernet (FCoE) is a technology that allows Fiber Channel (FC) protocols to run over Ethernet networks. As storage area networks (SANs) continue to grow and evolve, FCoE provides a solution that integrates the high-performance, low-latency capabilities of Fiber Channel with the widespread, cost-effective Ethernet infrastructure. The goal of FCoE is to simplify network architectures by consolidating storage and data networks onto a single Ethernet platform. This reduces the complexity and cost of maintaining separate infrastructures for storage and general network traffic. FCoE has gained significant traction in data centers and enterprise environments, where the demand for scalable, high-performance, and cost-effective solutions is increasing.

Fiber Channel, a protocol designed specifically for storage networks, offers high throughput, low latency, and robust reliability. Traditionally, Fiber Channel networks run on dedicated hardware, such as Fiber Channel switches and host bus adapters (HBAs), using specialized cabling like fiber optic cables. While this architecture has been highly effective for high-performance storage systems, it comes with several limitations, particularly in terms of cost, complexity, and the need for separate physical networks for storage and general data. Ethernet, on the other hand, is widely adopted, cheaper, and more flexible, but it does not inherently provide the low-latency, lossless communication required by high-performance storage applications.

FCoE solves this problem by enabling Fiber Channel frames to be encapsulated within Ethernet frames, thus allowing Fiber Channel traffic to be transmitted over a standard Ethernet network. By doing so, FCoE leverages the flexibility and cost-efficiency of Ethernet while maintaining the high performance of Fiber Channel. FCoE allows for the seamless integration of both data and storage traffic onto a single unified network, making it easier to manage and scale. This solution is particularly valuable in environments where data centers need to optimize their existing Ethernet infrastructure while ensuring that storage traffic remains high-priority and performance-driven.

One of the key features of FCoE is its ability to maintain the same high performance as traditional Fiber Channel networks. FCoE operates in a lossless Ethernet environment, which is achieved through the use of the Data Center Bridging (DCB) standard. DCB includes a set of protocols that provide the necessary mechanisms to ensure that Ethernet can be used for storage traffic without the risk of packet loss, which is crucial in Fiber Channel networks where data integrity and low latency are paramount. These DCB mechanisms include Priority Flow Control (PFC) and Enhanced Transmission Selection (ETS), which help manage network traffic and ensure that storage traffic is prioritized appropriately.

FCoE also reduces the number of cables and switches needed in a data center. Traditionally, data and storage networks would require separate physical connections, with separate cabling and network interfaces. By consolidating both types of traffic over a single Ethernet network, FCoE reduces the complexity of managing multiple networks and lowers operational costs. This is especially beneficial for organizations that are looking to simplify their infrastructure and reduce the number of physical devices they need to manage, thereby improving operational efficiency.

The integration of Fiber Channel over Ethernet into an existing network requires a few key changes to the infrastructure. First, Ethernet switches used for FCoE need to support Data Center Bridging (DCB). DCB-capable switches are required to manage the priority of traffic and prevent packet loss, ensuring that FCoE traffic is handled properly. Additionally, servers and storage devices need to be equipped with FCoE-capable network interface cards (NICs) or converged network adapters (CNAs). These adapters enable the encapsulation of Fiber Channel frames into Ethernet frames and allow servers to communicate with storage devices over the Ethernet network.

FCoE provides a highly scalable solution for storage networks. Since Ethernet is a widely used and standardized protocol, it is easier and more cost-effective to scale FCoE networks compared to traditional Fiber Channel networks. Expanding an FCoE network typically involves upgrading or adding additional Ethernet switches, which are more common and less expensive than traditional Fiber Channel switches. This scalability makes FCoE a compelling choice for businesses that need to grow their storage infrastructure without incurring the costs associated with dedicated Fiber Channel hardware.

Despite its many advantages, FCoE is not without its challenges. One of the primary concerns with FCoE is the need for a lossless Ethernet environment. Unlike traditional Ethernet, which can experience packet loss under heavy traffic conditions, FCoE requires a high degree of reliability to ensure that storage traffic is not disrupted. This is where Data Center Bridging (DCB) becomes essential, as it provides the mechanisms for ensuring the lossless transmission of data. Implementing DCB and ensuring that all components of the network are properly configured can require additional planning and investment, particularly in large-scale environments.

Another challenge is the fact that FCoE relies on converged network adapters (CNAs) to handle both Ethernet and Fiber Channel traffic. While CNAs are highly efficient, they may require updates or upgrades to existing network infrastructure, which could introduce additional complexity and cost. Additionally, there may be compatibility issues between legacy devices and newer FCoE-capable hardware. As such, organizations considering FCoE must carefully plan their migration strategy and ensure that they have the right hardware and software in place to fully support the new technology.

The implementation of FCoE can also require changes to the way network administrators manage and monitor the network. Traditional Fiber Channel networks use specialized management tools and protocols to monitor the performance and health of the network. In an FCoE environment, administrators need to be familiar with both Ethernet and Fiber Channel management systems to ensure that both types of traffic are being handled effectively. This may require training and additional expertise in both Ethernet networking and storage networking to properly configure, monitor, and troubleshoot the integrated network.

FCoE is particularly beneficial in environments where data storage needs to be tightly integrated with the general data network. In virtualized environments, where servers are typically using multiple storage resources, FCoE allows for the consolidation of both data and storage traffic over the same network, reducing the complexity and improving performance. Additionally, FCoE supports the use of advanced storage technologies such as Fibre Channel over IP (FCIP) and Fiber Channel-based replication, which provide extended reach and disaster recovery capabilities.

FCoE is a powerful technology that bridges the gap between traditional Fiber Channel networks and modern Ethernet infrastructures. By enabling Fiber Channel traffic to be carried over Ethernet networks, it provides a cost-effective and scalable solution for storage networks while maintaining the high-performance characteristics of Fiber Channel. As data centers continue to evolve and demand more efficient, unified solutions, FCoE offers a compelling alternative to traditional storage networking technologies. Its ability to simplify infrastructure, reduce costs, and improve scalability makes it a valuable tool for modern enterprises looking to optimize their storage environments.

# Storage Devices and Fiber Channel Connectivity

Fiber Channel technology has become the backbone of storage area networks (SANs) in enterprise environments due to its high performance, low-latency communication, and reliability in managing data traffic. One of the primary uses of Fiber Channel is connecting storage devices, such as disk arrays, tape libraries, and optical storage systems, to servers and other devices within the SAN. Understanding how storage devices connect to a Fiber Channel network and the key considerations for ensuring reliable, efficient communication is essential for building and maintaining robust storage infrastructure. In this chapter, we will explore the different types of storage devices commonly used in Fiber Channel networks, how they connect to the network, and the various factors that contribute to optimizing their performance and reliability.

At the core of a Fiber Channel network, storage devices play a crucial role in storing and retrieving data for servers, applications, and users. These devices can range from simple disk arrays to complex storage systems with advanced capabilities like virtualization, data replication, and tiered storage. Disk arrays are among the most common storage devices in Fiber Channel networks, offering high-capacity storage and redundancy through various RAID (Redundant Array of Independent Disks) configurations. These arrays use multiple disks to distribute data and parity information, ensuring that the data is protected against disk failure while providing high availability and fast access to stored information.

Tape libraries and optical storage systems, though less common in modern environments, are also used for archiving and backup purposes in Fiber Channel-connected networks. These devices are designed to provide long-term storage for large volumes of data that do not require frequent access. Tape libraries, for example, are widely used in disaster recovery and backup systems due to their cost-effectiveness for storing large amounts of data in a compact form. Fiber Channel connectivity ensures that these devices can be accessed reliably, even in remote locations, by allowing them to be integrated into the same SAN as other high-performance storage systems.

Connecting these storage devices to a Fiber Channel network is achieved through specialized hardware, such as Fiber Channel host bus adapters (HBAs) and Fiber Channel switches. The HBA is installed in the server or storage device and acts as the interface between the device and the Fiber Channel network. It converts data from the device into the Fiber Channel protocol, allowing it to communicate with other devices over the network. The HBA is essential for ensuring that the storage device can access the network and that data can be transmitted efficiently between servers and storage devices.

Fiber Channel switches are used to interconnect the various devices in the network, including servers and storage systems. These switches are responsible for routing data traffic between devices, ensuring that data is transmitted to the appropriate destination without unnecessary delay or congestion. The switch fabric, created by the interconnected switches, forms the backbone of the network, enabling devices to communicate with each other. A well-designed switch fabric ensures that data flows smoothly and efficiently, even as the network scales to accommodate more devices and higher data volumes.

The performance of storage devices in a Fiber Channel network depends on several factors, including the speed of the Fiber Channel links, the capacity of the storage devices, and the configuration of the network. Fiber Channel supports various speeds, ranging from 1 Gbps to 128 Gbps, with higher speeds offering greater throughput for data transfers. The choice of speed for a given network depends on the performance requirements of the storage devices and the applications they support. For example, high-performance applications like databases or virtualized environments may require faster Fiber Channel speeds to ensure that data is accessed quickly and reliably.

In addition to link speed, the capacity of the storage devices themselves is an important consideration. Storage arrays are available in various sizes, with larger arrays offering more storage capacity and higher performance. The performance of the storage device is also influenced by factors such as the type of disk used (e.g., HDD vs. SSD), the RAID configuration employed, and the level of redundancy built into the system. For instance, a storage array using solid-state drives (SSDs) will generally provide faster data access times compared to one using traditional hard disk drives (HDDs), making it suitable for high-performance applications. Similarly, RAID 10 configurations, which mirror data across multiple disks, offer a higher level of fault tolerance and performance than RAID 5, which uses a combination of striping and parity for redundancy.

As storage networks grow, the complexity of managing and optimizing the performance of the connected storage devices increases. Network administrators must consider factors such as the load on each device, the network traffic between devices, and the potential for bottlenecks in the system. Fiber Channel zoning is one technique used to manage this complexity. Zoning allows administrators to define logical groups of devices within the SAN, ensuring that only authorized devices can communicate with each other. By creating zones, administrators can reduce network congestion and improve security by isolating devices from one another as needed.

Additionally, the implementation of multipathing technology helps improve the redundancy and performance of storage devices in Fiber Channel networks. Multipathing involves creating multiple physical paths between servers and storage devices to provide redundancy and load balancing. If one path fails, the system can automatically switch to an alternate path, ensuring that the network remains operational even in the event of a failure. This is particularly important in environments where downtime is unacceptable, and ensuring uninterrupted access to storage is critical.

Another important aspect of Fiber Channel connectivity is the management of traffic flow between devices. The Fiber Channel protocol itself supports mechanisms such as flow control, which helps manage the rate at which data is transmitted to prevent congestion and ensure that devices can handle the incoming data without being overwhelmed. Advanced management software is often used to monitor the health and performance of storage devices, identify potential bottlenecks, and optimize traffic flow across the network. These tools allow administrators to track key metrics such as bandwidth utilization, latency, and error rates, providing valuable insights into the performance of the storage infrastructure.

The connection of storage devices to a Fiber Channel network also involves considerations for security. Fiber Channel networks are typically isolated from other network traffic, providing an inherent level of security by reducing exposure to external threats. However, additional security measures, such as encryption and authentication, may be required to protect sensitive data as it travels across the network. Zoning and access control policies are also essential for ensuring that only authorized devices can access specific storage resources, preventing unauthorized devices from gaining access to critical data.

As organizations continue to scale their storage networks, the integration of newer technologies such as cloud storage, virtualization, and software-defined storage (SDS) is becoming more prevalent. Fiber Channel connectivity plays a vital role in these technologies by providing a high-speed, reliable network for connecting on-premises storage with cloud storage resources and supporting virtualized environments that require high-performance access to storage. The ability to seamlessly integrate Fiber Channel with these emerging technologies ensures that businesses can meet the growing demands of modern data storage and management.

Storage devices and Fiber Channel connectivity are central to the design and operation of efficient, high-performance SANs. By connecting storage devices through Fiber Channel, organizations can ensure fast, reliable, and secure access to data, while also providing the scalability and redundancy required for mission-critical applications. Whether dealing with traditional disk arrays, tape libraries, or the latest solid-state storage solutions, Fiber Channel connectivity provides the foundation for building robust, high-performance storage networks that meet the needs of modern enterprises.

# Implementing and Managing Fiber Channel HBAs

Fiber Channel Host Bus Adapters (HBAs) are critical components in connecting servers to Fiber Channel networks, enabling data transfer between storage devices and hosts in storage area networks (SANs). These specialized adapters facilitate high-speed, low-latency communication and are designed to provide reliable access to storage resources. The implementation and management of Fiber Channel HBAs are essential to ensure the optimal performance, security, and scalability of a Fiber Channel SAN. Understanding how to implement and manage these adapters, as well as the considerations involved, is crucial for network administrators and engineers working in data-intensive environments.

An HBA is a hardware device installed in a server or storage device that connects the host to the Fiber Channel network. It serves as the interface between the server's internal components and the external SAN, converting the host's data into the appropriate Fiber Channel protocol. The HBA is responsible for transmitting data packets to and from storage devices across the SAN, ensuring that data can be accessed and written quickly and reliably. Without HBAs, a server would not be able to communicate with a SAN using Fiber Channel, making these devices essential for the operation of high-performance storage networks.

When implementing Fiber Channel HBAs, one of the first steps is to determine the appropriate type of HBA for the server or storage device. Fiber Channel HBAs are available in different speeds, typically ranging from 1 Gbps to 128 Gbps, depending on the performance requirements of the network. The choice of HBA speed depends on the bandwidth needed by the server and the overall requirements of the SAN. High-performance applications, such as databases or virtualization platforms, may require faster HBAs to ensure that data can be accessed quickly and without delays. For smaller environments or less performance-demanding applications, slower HBAs may be sufficient. The scalability of the network must also be considered when selecting HBAs, as future growth may necessitate faster adapters.

Fiber Channel HBAs can be either internal or external, depending on the type of server or storage device. Internal HBAs are typically used in blade servers or rack-mounted servers and are installed directly onto the server's motherboard or through PCIe slots. External HBAs, on the other hand, are used when connecting servers to SANs that require external adapters. These HBAs are usually connected via cables or fiber optics to the storage devices in the SAN. Regardless of the form factor, all Fiber Channel HBAs share the same fundamental purpose: enabling high-speed communication between the server and the storage network.

The process of implementing Fiber Channel HBAs involves more than just selecting the correct hardware. It also requires configuring the adapters to ensure that they are properly connected to the SAN and that the data can flow between the server and storage devices without issues. This configuration typically involves installing the necessary drivers and software for the HBA, which allows the server's operating system to recognize the adapter and enable communication with the Fiber Channel network. The installation of drivers is critical to the functioning of the HBA, as it ensures that the device can interface correctly with both the server and the SAN. In some cases, specialized management software from the HBA manufacturer may also be required to monitor and control the HBA's operation.

Once the HBA is installed and the drivers are configured, the next step is to connect the HBA to the Fiber Channel network. This involves connecting the adapter to the appropriate ports on the SAN switches and configuring the zoning settings to ensure that the server can communicate with the correct storage devices. Zoning is a key aspect of Fiber Channel SANs, as it defines which devices are allowed to communicate with each other. By setting up zones, administrators can control traffic flow and prevent unauthorized access to storage resources. The HBA must be included in the correct zone to ensure that it can access the appropriate storage volumes.

Managing Fiber Channel HBAs involves monitoring their performance, ensuring they are functioning correctly, and maintaining them over time. Proper management is essential for ensuring that the SAN continues to operate efficiently and that data is transmitted without delays or errors. One of the most important aspects of managing HBAs is monitoring their health and performance. This can be done using the management tools provided by the HBA manufacturer or through third-party network management software. These tools allow administrators to track key metrics such as bandwidth utilization, error rates, and link status, helping them to identify potential issues before they affect the overall performance of the network.

One of the most common issues that can arise with Fiber Channel HBAs is link failure. If an HBA experiences a failure, the server may lose access to the SAN, leading to downtime and potential data loss. To prevent this, many Fiber Channel SANs are configured with redundancy and failover capabilities. Redundancy ensures that there are multiple paths for data to travel, so if one path fails, the data can be rerouted through another path without causing disruption. This is typically accomplished using multipathing software, which automatically detects link failures and switches to an alternate path. Multipathing provides increased reliability and ensures that the SAN remains operational even in the event of hardware failure.

Another important consideration when managing Fiber Channel HBAs is performance tuning. Over time, as the SAN grows and more devices are added, the performance of the HBA may degrade due to increased traffic or network congestion. Regular performance monitoring is essential to identify bottlenecks or other issues that may affect the speed and efficiency of data transfer. Adjustments to the configuration, such as increasing link speeds, adding more HBAs, or optimizing zoning settings, may be necessary to ensure that the network continues to meet performance requirements.

Security is also a crucial aspect of managing Fiber Channel HBAs. While Fiber Channel networks are inherently more secure than traditional IP-based networks due to their isolated nature, it is still important to implement security measures to protect sensitive data. This includes setting up access control policies and ensuring that only authorized devices are allowed to connect to the network. Encryption can also be used to protect data as it travels over the SAN, ensuring that it remains secure even in the event of a breach. In addition, administrators must ensure that the HBA's firmware is up to date to protect against security vulnerabilities.

Fiber Channel HBAs are vital components in building high-performance, reliable SANs. The process of implementing and managing these adapters involves selecting the right hardware, configuring the devices, and continuously monitoring and maintaining their performance. By ensuring that HBAs are properly installed and managed, administrators can guarantee that their SANs operate efficiently and that data is transferred quickly and securely. As data demands continue to grow and storage networks become increasingly complex, the role of Fiber Channel HBAs in enabling fast, reliable access to storage resources will remain integral to the success of modern enterprise IT infrastructures.

# SAN Cabling and Fiber Channel Transmission Media

In a Storage Area Network (SAN), the cabling and transmission media play a pivotal role in determining the speed, reliability, and overall performance of data transmission across the network. Fiber Channel (FC) technology, specifically designed for storage networks, relies heavily on its transmission media to provide high-speed, low-latency communication between servers, storage devices, and other components within the SAN. Understanding the different types of cabling and the characteristics of the transmission media used in Fiber Channel networks is crucial for ensuring that the network operates efficiently, maintains high performance, and supports future growth.

Fiber Channel networks primarily use two types of transmission media: optical fiber and copper cabling. The choice of cabling depends on the specific requirements of the network, including factors such as distance, performance, cost, and environmental considerations. Fiber optic cables are typically used for longer-distance connections and high-performance networks, while copper cables are commonly used in shorter-range connections or where cost constraints are a primary consideration. Each of these media types has distinct characteristics that impact the design, scalability, and performance of the SAN.

Optical fiber is the most widely used transmission medium in Fiber Channel networks due to its ability to transmit data over long distances without significant signal degradation. Fiber optic cables are made from strands of glass or plastic that carry light signals, which are much faster and more efficient than electrical signals used in copper cables. Because light signals are not affected by electromagnetic interference (EMI) or radio frequency interference (RFI), optical fiber offers a higher level of reliability and performance, especially in environments with high levels of electrical noise or where signals need to travel over significant distances. Fiber optic cables are essential for connecting distant components in large-scale SANs, where servers, storage devices, and switches may be located in different parts of a data center or even across different geographic locations.

Fiber optic cables are typically categorized by their core size and the type of light transmission used. Single-mode fiber (SMF) and multi-mode fiber (MMF) are the two main types of fiber optic cables used in Fiber Channel networks. Single-mode fiber has a smaller core diameter and is designed to carry a single light path, making it ideal for long-distance communication. It can transmit data over several kilometers, depending on the type of equipment and the wavelength used. Multi-mode fiber, on the other hand, has a larger core diameter and supports multiple light paths, making it suitable for shorter distances, typically within a data center. Multi-mode fiber can transmit data over distances of up to 500 meters, depending on the specific requirements of the network. The choice between single-mode and multi-mode fiber depends on the distance and performance requirements of the SAN, with single-mode fiber being preferred for long-range connections and multi-mode fiber being more suitable for short-range, high-bandwidth applications.

While fiber optic cables offer superior performance for long-distance communication, copper cabling also has its place in Fiber Channel networks, especially for short-range connections. Copper cables, such as coaxial cables and twisted pair cables, are often used in situations where the cost of fiber optic cabling may be prohibitive or where the transmission distance is relatively short. Copper cables are less expensive than optical fiber and are widely available, making them a cost-effective option for environments where high-speed data transmission is required over shorter distances. However, copper cabling has limitations in terms of speed, distance, and susceptibility to electromagnetic interference compared to fiber optic cables. In Fiber Channel networks, copper cables are typically used for shorter distances, such as within a server rack or between closely located devices within a SAN.

When it comes to Fiber Channel transmission media, the type of connector used also plays an important role in ensuring a reliable connection between devices. Fiber optic cables require specific types of connectors, including LC, SC, and MTP/MPO connectors, each of which has different characteristics in terms of size, ease of use, and performance. LC connectors are small form-factor connectors that are commonly used in data centers due to their high density and ease of installation. SC connectors, on the other hand, are slightly larger and are often used in applications that require a more secure connection. MTP/MPO connectors are typically used in high-density applications and offer the ability to connect multiple fibers at once, simplifying cable management in large-scale SAN environments. The choice of connector depends on the specific needs of the SAN, including space constraints, performance requirements, and the overall design of the network.

The physical topology of the Fiber Channel network also plays a significant role in determining the cabling requirements. A Fiber Channel network can be designed using several topologies, such as point-to-point, arbitrated loop, and switched fabric, with switched fabric being the most commonly used in large-scale SAN environments. The switch fabric topology involves connecting multiple devices, such as servers and storage devices, to a network of Fiber Channel switches. This topology requires extensive cabling and careful planning to ensure that data can flow efficiently between devices. The switches act as the central communication points in the network, routing data between devices based on their physical connections and logical configurations. Fiber optic cables are typically used to connect the devices to the switches, ensuring high-speed data transfer and minimizing signal loss.

The implementation of Fiber Channel cabling in a SAN also involves considerations for scalability, redundancy, and fault tolerance. As SANs grow and expand, the cabling infrastructure must be able to support the increasing number of devices and the higher data throughput required by modern applications. Redundancy is a key design consideration in Fiber Channel networks, as it ensures that there are alternate paths for data transmission in the event of a failure. The use of dual paths and redundant cabling ensures that the SAN remains operational even if one link or cable fails, minimizing the risk of downtime and data loss. This redundancy can be achieved by using multiple switches, HBAs, and cables, providing multiple physical paths for data to travel across the network.

In addition to physical redundancy, network performance can be further optimized by implementing advanced techniques such as link aggregation and multipathing. Link aggregation allows multiple physical links to be combined into a single logical link, increasing the available bandwidth and improving the overall performance of the SAN. Multipathing, on the other hand, involves the use of multiple data paths between devices to provide fault tolerance and load balancing. These techniques, when combined with the right cabling and transmission media, help ensure that the SAN performs at optimal levels and remains resilient to failure.

Managing and maintaining the cabling infrastructure in a Fiber Channel network is an ongoing task. Proper cable management is essential to prevent issues such as signal interference, congestion, or physical damage to the cables. Cable trays, racks, and other management tools are used to organize and secure the cables, ensuring that they are easy to maintain and replace when necessary. Regular inspection of the cabling infrastructure is necessary to ensure that there are no physical issues, such as bent cables or loose connectors, that could compromise the network's performance.

The choice of cabling and transmission media in a Fiber Channel network is a critical factor in ensuring the network's performance, scalability, and reliability. By selecting the appropriate media for the specific needs of the SAN, network administrators can create a robust, high-performance storage environment that supports the growing demands of modern applications. Whether using fiber optic cables for long-distance communication or copper cables for short-range connections, the right transmission media is essential for achieving the high-speed, low-latency data transfer that is characteristic of Fiber Channel networks.

# Performance Optimization in Fiber Channel Networks

Fiber Channel networks play a pivotal role in modern data centers by providing high-performance, low-latency communication for storage systems. As organizations continue to generate and process vast amounts of data, optimizing the performance of Fiber Channel networks is crucial to ensure fast, efficient, and reliable data access. Performance optimization in Fiber Channel networks involves a combination of network design, configuration, and management techniques that ensure the infrastructure can handle high volumes of data traffic while minimizing bottlenecks, congestion, and downtime. Achieving optimal performance in Fiber Channel networks requires careful planning and continuous monitoring to adapt to the evolving needs of modern IT environments.

One of the key factors in optimizing the performance of a Fiber Channel network is ensuring that the physical network infrastructure is designed to handle the necessary data throughput. Fiber Channel operates over different types of cabling, including optical fiber and copper, each with its own performance characteristics. The choice of transmission medium plays a critical role in determining the network's overall bandwidth and latency. Optical fiber cables, especially single-mode fiber, offer high-speed data transmission over long distances with minimal signal loss, making them ideal for high-performance environments. By ensuring that the network is equipped with the appropriate cabling for the required distance and performance level, administrators can avoid performance degradation and ensure smooth data transfer across the network.

Another important consideration in optimizing Fiber Channel network performance is the choice of hardware components, particularly the switches, host bus adapters (HBAs), and storage devices. Fiber Channel switches are responsible for directing traffic between devices and ensuring that data is transmitted efficiently. The performance of the switches directly impacts the overall speed and reliability of the network. High-quality, high-capacity switches that are capable of handling large volumes of data traffic without introducing latency are essential for maintaining optimal performance. The number of switches, their configuration, and their ability to support advanced features such as Quality of Service (QoS) and multipathing can have a significant impact on the overall performance of the network.

HBAs are another critical component in Fiber Channel network performance optimization. These adapters serve as the interface between the servers and the Fiber Channel network, enabling data to be transmitted between storage devices and the host system. The speed and capabilities of the HBA directly affect the throughput and responsiveness of the network. Higher-speed HBAs, such as 16 Gbps or 32 Gbps models, offer better performance and can handle more data traffic, reducing bottlenecks at the server level. Additionally, ensuring that the HBAs are properly configured to work with the Fiber Channel network's switches and storage devices is crucial to maximizing performance.

Storage devices themselves must also be optimized for performance in a Fiber Channel network. This involves choosing the right type of storage (e.g., solid-state drives (SSDs) or hard disk drives (HDDs)), configuring them with appropriate RAID levels for redundancy and performance, and ensuring that they are properly connected to the network. In high-performance environments, SSDs are typically preferred because they offer significantly faster data access speeds compared to traditional HDDs. Additionally, using advanced storage techniques such as storage tiering, where frequently accessed data is stored on faster storage devices, can improve overall system performance by reducing latency.

Managing network traffic is another key aspect of optimizing Fiber Channel network performance. Network congestion can occur when there is too much data traffic for the network to handle, leading to delays, packet loss, and slower performance. To prevent congestion, administrators can implement techniques such as zoning and traffic prioritization. Zoning allows administrators to create logical groupings of devices within the network, ensuring that devices only communicate with those they need to. This reduces the overall amount of traffic that needs to be handled by the switches and helps to avoid network bottlenecks. Traffic prioritization, on the other hand, ensures that critical data, such as storage traffic, is given higher priority over less important data. This helps to ensure that performance-sensitive applications are not slowed down by non-critical traffic.

Another technique used to optimize Fiber Channel network performance is link aggregation. Link aggregation involves combining multiple physical links into a single logical connection, which increases the available bandwidth between devices. This technique allows the network to handle more traffic without overloading any single link, improving overall throughput and reducing the risk of congestion. Link aggregation can be particularly useful in environments where data transfer demands are high, such as in virtualized environments or large-scale database applications. By providing additional bandwidth, link aggregation ensures that the network can handle peak traffic loads and continue to perform at optimal levels.

Multipathing is another performance optimization technique used in Fiber Channel networks. Multipathing involves creating multiple physical paths between servers and storage devices, allowing data to be transmitted over alternate routes in the event of a failure. This redundancy not only improves network reliability but also enhances performance by enabling load balancing. With multipathing, data traffic can be distributed across multiple paths, preventing any single path from becoming overloaded and ensuring that data is transmitted as efficiently as possible. Multipathing also ensures that the network remains operational even if one of the paths fails, minimizing downtime and ensuring continuous access to storage resources.

Monitoring and management tools play a vital role in optimizing Fiber Channel network performance. By continuously monitoring key performance indicators (KPIs) such as latency, throughput, and error rates, administrators can identify potential issues before they impact the network. Monitoring tools provide real-time visibility into the health of the network, allowing administrators to detect bottlenecks, link failures, and other issues that may affect performance. These tools can also help administrators track the performance of individual components, such as switches, HBAs, and storage devices, and make adjustments to optimize the network's overall performance.

Capacity planning is another essential aspect of performance optimization. As data traffic and storage demands grow, the network must be able to scale to accommodate the increased load. Regular assessments of the network's capacity and performance ensure that the infrastructure can handle future growth. Upgrading components, such as switches or storage devices, or adding additional links to the network may be necessary to maintain optimal performance as data volumes increase. Proper capacity planning helps to prevent performance degradation as the network scales and ensures that the SAN can continue to meet the growing demands of modern applications.

In addition to these technical measures, optimizing Fiber Channel network performance also requires a proactive approach to maintenance and troubleshooting. Regular firmware and software updates for switches, HBAs, and other components ensure that the network remains up to date and that any known performance issues or security vulnerabilities are addressed. Troubleshooting tools can help administrators quickly diagnose and resolve performance issues, minimizing downtime and ensuring that the network operates at peak efficiency.

Optimizing the performance of Fiber Channel networks is essential for ensuring that storage systems can meet the growing demands of modern applications. By carefully designing the network infrastructure, selecting high-performance components, managing traffic effectively, and implementing techniques such as link aggregation, multipathing, and zoning, administrators can ensure that the SAN operates efficiently and reliably. Performance optimization is an ongoing process that requires continuous monitoring, regular maintenance, and proactive planning to address future growth and challenges. Through these efforts, organizations can create high-performance, scalable Fiber Channel networks that support the ever-increasing data requirements of today's enterprise environments.

# Data Integrity and Error Handling in Fiber Channel Networks

In modern storage area networks (SANs), data integrity and error handling are paramount for ensuring the reliability, performance, and security of data transmissions. Fiber Channel (FC) technology, widely used in high-performance and high-availability environments, is built with mechanisms that guarantee data is transferred accurately, even under heavy loads. Fiber Channel is designed to detect and correct errors, ensuring that data remains intact as it travels across the network. With data being one of the most valuable assets in any organization, the ability to prevent data corruption and handle transmission errors is a crucial feature of Fiber Channel networks. The following discusses how Fiber Channel networks maintain data integrity and the various error handling techniques employed to ensure that data is delivered reliably.

One of the key features of Fiber Channel networks is their inherent ability to maintain data integrity during transmission. Data integrity refers to the accuracy, consistency, and trustworthiness of data as it is stored or transmitted. In Fiber Channel, the protocol is designed to detect and correct errors at both the physical and protocol layers. For instance, Fiber Channel uses cyclic redundancy checks (CRC) to detect errors in data packets. A CRC is a hash value generated from the data and used to ensure that the data has not been altered or corrupted during transmission. If the calculated CRC value at the receiving end does not match the one sent with the data, the data is considered corrupt, and the transmission is rejected. This provides an automatic mechanism for detecting transmission errors that could compromise the integrity of the data.

In addition to CRCs, Fiber Channel uses other error detection mechanisms at different layers of the protocol. These mechanisms help ensure that data can be verified for accuracy and consistency at each stage of its journey through the network. For example, the Fiber Channel protocol includes a built-in mechanism called the Frame Check Sequence (FCS), which is similar to CRCs and is used to detect any discrepancies in the data. The FCS is calculated at the source end of the communication and is appended to the data. When the data is received at the destination, the FCS is recalculated and compared to the original value. If the values do not match, the receiver knows that the data has been corrupted during transmission and requests that the data be retransmitted.

Error handling in Fiber Channel networks is not limited to the detection of errors. It also involves strategies for correcting and recovering from those errors to minimize the impact on data availability and network performance. One of the primary methods for handling errors in Fiber Channel networks is the use of automatic retransmission. When a corrupted frame is detected, the protocol ensures that the affected frame is retransmitted without manual intervention. This is essential in environments where uptime is critical, such as in data centers, where downtime can result in significant operational disruptions. The retransmission process ensures that any errors in data transmission are corrected quickly and without manual involvement, reducing the likelihood of data corruption and maintaining network performance.

Another important aspect of error handling in Fiber Channel networks is the use of flow control. Fiber Channel networks implement flow control mechanisms to prevent network congestion and the resulting errors that may arise due to overwhelmed network components. Flow control allows the receiver to communicate to the sender whether it is ready to accept more data. If the receiver is overloaded or busy processing data, it can signal the sender to pause transmission until it is ready to continue. This prevents the loss of data and ensures that the network is not flooded with more data than it can handle at any given moment. By managing the flow of data between devices, Fiber Channel networks can reduce the likelihood of errors that result from network congestion, such as data packet loss or delays in transmission.

Fiber Channel also incorporates features such as acknowledgments and timeouts, which play a crucial role in error recovery. When data is transmitted across the network, the sender expects to receive an acknowledgment from the receiver indicating that the data was successfully received. If the acknowledgment is not received within a specified timeout period, the sender will assume that the transmission has failed and will automatically retry sending the data. This retry mechanism ensures that data is not lost in transit due to network issues or temporary interruptions. In some cases, the receiver may request a retransmission of the data if it detects an error or if the data does not meet the expected checksum criteria. These automatic retry and acknowledgment mechanisms are vital for maintaining data integrity, especially in large and complex networks where human intervention is not always feasible.

The error-handling capabilities of Fiber Channel networks are designed to provide high availability and fault tolerance. One of the ways this is achieved is through redundancy and the use of multiple paths between devices in the network. Fiber Channel SANs can be configured with multiple redundant links between storage devices and servers. This ensures that if one path becomes unavailable due to a failure, the data can still be transmitted via an alternate path. Multipathing, a technique used in Fiber Channel networks, allows for the automatic selection of an alternate data path if one path fails, ensuring continuous data availability. By using multiple redundant paths, Fiber Channel networks can minimize the risk of data loss or corruption caused by path failures, ensuring high availability of storage resources.

Monitoring and management are also essential aspects of ensuring data integrity and error handling in Fiber Channel networks. Network administrators use specialized management software to monitor the health and performance of Fiber Channel switches, HBAs, and storage devices. These tools allow administrators to track the occurrence of errors, such as CRC failures or FCS mismatches, and provide real-time alerts when issues arise. By actively monitoring the network, administrators can quickly identify and resolve potential issues before they escalate and cause significant disruptions. Regular audits of the network's error-handling mechanisms also help identify any weaknesses or vulnerabilities in the system and ensure that best practices for error recovery are followed.

Fiber Channel networks also provide features for isolating errors and preventing them from affecting the broader network. For example, zoning allows network administrators to create logical groupings of devices that can communicate only with each other, which helps to prevent the propagation of errors from one device to another. By controlling the flow of data and limiting the scope of potential errors, zoning helps reduce the impact of failures on the overall performance of the network. Additionally, advanced diagnostic tools help administrators isolate issues to specific components, such as switches, HBAs, or cables, making it easier to identify the root cause of an error and address it promptly.

The importance of data integrity and error handling in Fiber Channel networks cannot be overstated. As businesses become increasingly reliant on data for critical operations, ensuring that data is transmitted accurately and securely is essential. Fiber Channel networks provide robust mechanisms for error detection, automatic retransmission, and fault tolerance, all of which are crucial for maintaining the integrity of the data flowing through the network. By employing a combination of hardware and software solutions, including flow control, acknowledgments, timeouts, redundancy, and monitoring tools, Fiber Channel networks ensure that data remains intact and available, even in the face of errors or network issues. These error-handling capabilities provide a foundation for high-performance, high-reliability storage solutions that businesses can depend on to support their most important applications.

## Security in Fiber Channel Networks

Fiber Channel networks are crucial for the management and transmission of large volumes of data in environments where performance, reliability, and availability are paramount. However, like any other network infrastructure, Fiber Channel networks must also be designed with security in mind to protect against unauthorized access, data breaches, and potential disruptions. The inherent security risks associated with data storage and network traffic make it essential for administrators to implement robust security measures within Fiber Channel networks to safeguard sensitive data and maintain the integrity of the network. Understanding the security mechanisms available in Fiber Channel, as well as how to implement them effectively, is crucial for ensuring that a SAN (Storage Area Network) operates securely and efficiently.

Fiber Channel networks are often deployed in high-performance environments, such as data centers, where critical applications and sensitive data are stored and accessed. The primary function of Fiber Channel is to provide fast, low-latency communication between storage devices and servers. Because of the high value of the data being transmitted, these networks are a frequent target for cyber threats, making it vital to protect the integrity of the data and the availability of the network. Fiber Channel provides several mechanisms that can be utilized to enhance the security of the network and protect data from unauthorized access and tampering.

One of the key security features of Fiber Channel networks is the use of zoning. Zoning is a method used to segment the network into isolated areas, ensuring that only authorized devices can communicate with each other. Zoning creates logical boundaries within the Fiber Channel fabric, allowing administrators to define which devices can access specific storage resources. This segmentation helps minimize the risk of unauthorized access and ensures that devices only interact with the storage systems they are permitted to. There are two primary types of zoning: port-based zoning and World Wide Name (WWN)-based zoning. Port-based zoning controls access by using the physical ports on the switches, while WWN-based zoning uses the unique identifiers of the devices to determine which devices can communicate with each other. WWN-based zoning offers greater flexibility, as it is not tied to specific physical ports, and devices can be moved around without reconfiguring the zoning.

Fiber Channel networks also rely on authentication to secure access to the network and prevent unauthorized devices from joining the fabric. Authentication mechanisms help ensure that only trusted devices are allowed to participate in the network. Fiber Channel Security Protocol (FC-SP) is the most widely adopted standard for securing Fiber Channel networks. FC-SP provides an authentication framework that ensures devices connecting to the network are properly authenticated before being granted access. This authentication process helps mitigate the risk of rogue devices being connected to the network and accessing sensitive data. By using FC-SP, administrators can define trust relationships between devices and enforce security policies that prevent unauthorized access to the SAN.

Encryption is another critical component of securing Fiber Channel networks. While Fiber Channel provides inherent security by isolating the storage traffic from the rest of the network, encryption adds an extra layer of protection by ensuring that data is unreadable to unauthorized parties. Fiber Channel networks can use encryption protocols to encrypt data as it is transmitted across the network, making it much harder for attackers to intercept and read the data. This is especially important when sensitive data is being transmitted between servers and storage devices, as it ensures that even if an attacker gains access to the network, they will not be able to decipher the data. Many Fiber Channel switches and storage devices support the implementation of encryption either through hardware or software, depending on the specific needs of the network.

In addition to encryption, Fiber Channel networks can also implement access control lists (ACLs) to further restrict access to sensitive data and resources. ACLs allow administrators to define granular access policies that specify which users or devices are permitted to access certain parts of the network. By setting up ACLs, administrators can ensure that only authorized personnel or systems can access specific storage resources, enhancing security by reducing the number of users who have access to sensitive data. ACLs are particularly important in environments where data segregation is required, such as in multi-tenant data centers, where each tenant's data must be kept separate from others.

Fiber Channel networks also utilize integrity-checking mechanisms to ensure that data is not tampered with during transmission. One of the primary integrity mechanisms is the Frame Check Sequence (FCS), which is a part of the Fiber Channel protocol. The FCS is a mathematical calculation applied to each data frame before it is transmitted. When the frame reaches its destination, the receiver performs the same calculation to verify that the data has not been altered in transit. If the FCS does not match, the frame is discarded, and a retransmission is requested. This mechanism helps prevent the manipulation of data during transmission, ensuring that the data remains intact and reliable.

Another security concern in Fiber Channel networks is the physical security of the network components, such as the switches, cables, and HBAs (Host Bus Adapters). Physical access to these components must be carefully controlled to prevent unauthorized tampering or damage to the network. Switches, in particular, can be targets for attackers attempting to gain control over the network, so it is important to place them in secure, access-controlled locations. Furthermore, cabling should be carefully managed to prevent unauthorized devices from connecting to the network. Fiber Channel switches can also be configured with security features, such as port security, which limits the number of devices that can connect to each port and prevents unauthorized devices from being added to the network.

Monitoring and logging are essential aspects of securing a Fiber Channel network. By continuously monitoring the network for signs of suspicious activity, administrators can quickly detect and respond to potential security threats. Many Fiber Channel switches and management tools offer logging capabilities that track events such as failed login attempts, unauthorized access attempts, and other anomalous activities. These logs can be analyzed to identify potential security risks and ensure that the network remains secure. Regular audits of the network's security settings and configurations can also help identify weaknesses and ensure that the network is protected from emerging threats.

Security in Fiber Channel networks is a multi-faceted approach that involves implementing a range of tools and strategies to protect data from unauthorized access, corruption, and tampering. By leveraging zoning, authentication, encryption, access control, and integrity-checking mechanisms, administrators can build a robust security framework that ensures the confidentiality, integrity, and availability of data in a Fiber Channel network. As organizations increasingly rely on storage networks to support critical applications and manage vast amounts of sensitive data, the importance of security in Fiber Channel networks continues to grow. Protecting data from external and internal threats is crucial to maintaining the trust of customers and ensuring the smooth operation of the business. With the right security measures in place, Fiber Channel networks can provide a secure, high-performance foundation for the modern enterprise.

# SAN Storage Virtualization and Fiber Channel

Storage virtualization has become a critical component in modern data centers, providing organizations with the ability to manage and scale their storage resources more efficiently. It allows administrators to create a unified view of storage resources, abstracting the underlying physical infrastructure and enabling easier management, provisioning, and scaling. Fiber Channel networks, with their high-performance, low-latency communication, are ideally suited for supporting storage virtualization in environments where fast, reliable access to data is essential. The integration of storage virtualization with Fiber Channel enhances the flexibility, scalability, and efficiency of storage area networks (SANs), enabling businesses to optimize their storage environments and better meet the demands of modern applications.

At its core, storage virtualization involves abstracting the physical storage devices into a single, logical pool of storage resources that can be dynamically allocated to servers and applications as needed. This abstraction layer hides the complexity of the underlying storage infrastructure and simplifies management tasks. Virtualized storage can take many forms, from virtual disks that are made available to virtual machines to larger-scale virtualized storage arrays that aggregate multiple physical devices into a single logical unit. The key advantage of storage virtualization is that it decouples the logical view of storage from the physical devices, allowing for greater flexibility in how storage resources are provisioned, managed, and utilized.

In a Fiber Channel SAN, storage virtualization can be particularly effective because of the high bandwidth and low latency provided by Fiber Channel technology. Fiber Channel networks are known for their reliability, high-speed data transfer, and scalability, which makes them ideal for virtualized environments that require fast and efficient access to large volumes of data. The low-latency nature of Fiber Channel ensures that the virtualized storage environment operates efficiently, even when multiple servers or applications are accessing data simultaneously.

Fiber Channel technology, with its ability to support high-speed connections and non-blocking communication, enables seamless access to virtualized storage resources. By connecting storage devices, servers, and switches in a Fiber Channel network, organizations can create a centralized pool of storage that is shared across multiple servers. This pooling of storage resources allows for better utilization and optimization of storage capacity, as administrators can dynamically allocate storage based on demand without the need for manual intervention. The use of Fiber Channel switches within the SAN fabric enables efficient routing of data between servers and storage devices, ensuring that virtualized storage resources are accessed quickly and reliably.

Incorporating Fiber Channel into storage virtualization also offers a number of benefits when it comes to scalability. As businesses grow and data storage needs increase, Fiber Channel networks provide the bandwidth and flexibility to scale storage environments efficiently. By adding more storage devices, switches, or servers to the network, organizations can expand their virtualized storage infrastructure without significant disruption to operations. Fiber Channel's high scalability allows for seamless integration of new storage resources, enabling businesses to keep up with increasing data demands while maintaining consistent performance across the network.

Another advantage of integrating Fiber Channel with storage virtualization is improved data availability and fault tolerance. Fiber Channel SANs can be configured with redundancy and failover mechanisms to ensure that virtualized storage resources remain available, even in the event of a failure. Multipathing, for example, allows for multiple physical paths between servers and storage devices, providing an alternate route for data in case one path fails. This redundancy ensures continuous access to virtualized storage resources, reducing the risk of downtime and data loss. Additionally, the use of Fiber Channel switches with built-in redundancy further enhances the resilience of the storage network, allowing data to continue flowing even if one switch or path fails.

Security is another critical consideration when implementing storage virtualization in Fiber Channel networks. Virtualized storage environments must be protected from unauthorized access and data breaches, especially in industries where sensitive data is stored and processed. Fiber Channel networks provide inherent security features, such as zoning and access control, which help isolate different parts of the network and ensure that only authorized devices can access specific storage resources. Zoning allows administrators to segment the network into logical zones, restricting communication to only those devices that belong to the same zone. This isolation helps prevent unauthorized access to sensitive data and reduces the risk of data exposure.

In addition to zoning, storage virtualization in Fiber Channel SANs can be further secured through encryption and authentication mechanisms. Fiber Channel Security Protocol (FC-SP) is a widely used standard that provides an authentication framework to secure communication between devices in the SAN. FC-SP ensures that only authorized devices can join the network and access storage resources, providing an additional layer of protection against potential security threats. Encryption can also be applied to protect data in transit across the Fiber Channel network, ensuring that sensitive information remains confidential even if intercepted by malicious actors.

The management of virtualized storage in Fiber Channel networks also benefits from centralized management tools. These tools allow administrators to monitor the performance and health of both physical and virtualized storage resources from a single interface. Administrators can allocate storage, monitor usage, and optimize the performance of the virtualized storage environment with ease. This centralized approach simplifies administrative tasks, reducing the complexity of managing large-scale storage infrastructures. Additionally, many of these management tools offer advanced features such as automated provisioning and dynamic resource allocation, which further streamline the process of managing virtualized storage.

One of the key challenges when implementing storage virtualization in Fiber Channel SANs is ensuring that the virtualized storage environment remains responsive and performs well under heavy loads. As multiple virtual machines or applications access shared storage resources, the demand on the underlying network infrastructure can increase significantly. To address this, administrators must carefully monitor the performance of the Fiber Channel network, ensuring that bandwidth is allocated efficiently and that data flows smoothly between devices. Techniques such as load balancing, traffic prioritization, and the use of high-performance switches can help mitigate performance degradation in virtualized environments.

Storage virtualization also offers opportunities for improved disaster recovery and data protection. By centralizing storage resources and enabling the dynamic allocation of storage capacity, organizations can implement more efficient backup and replication strategies. Virtualized storage allows for more flexible disaster recovery solutions, such as snapshot-based backups and real-time data replication to remote sites. Fiber Channel SANs provide the high-speed connectivity required to support these data protection strategies, ensuring that virtualized storage can be backed up and recovered quickly in the event of a failure.

Storage virtualization in Fiber Channel networks is a powerful tool that allows organizations to optimize their storage resources, improve scalability, and ensure high availability. By abstracting the underlying storage infrastructure, virtualization enables businesses to manage their data more efficiently and meet the growing demands of modern applications. When combined with the high-speed, low-latency performance of Fiber Channel, storage virtualization enhances the overall flexibility and resilience of the SAN, making it an essential component of modern IT environments. With proper implementation and management, storage virtualization and Fiber Channel can provide the foundation for a highly efficient, secure, and scalable storage infrastructure that meets the needs of today's data-driven world.

# Key Benefits of SAN for Enterprise Storage Solutions

Storage Area Networks (SANs) have become an essential component of enterprise storage infrastructures due to their ability to provide fast, reliable, and scalable storage solutions. SANs offer organizations the ability to centralize and manage their storage resources more efficiently, which is crucial in today's data-driven world, where rapid access to large volumes of data is essential for business operations. By connecting servers and storage devices over a high-speed network, SANs offer a host of benefits that can significantly improve performance, scalability, and data management. These advantages make SANs particularly well-suited for enterprise environments that require high availability, fast data access, and robust disaster recovery capabilities.

One of the primary benefits of SANs is their ability to improve storage utilization and efficiency. In traditional direct-attached storage (DAS) configurations, each server typically has its own dedicated storage, leading to inefficiencies in storage utilization. Servers may be underutilized, or storage resources may be wasted if a server does not require the full capacity of its attached storage. SANs eliminate this inefficiency by allowing multiple servers to share a centralized pool of storage, enabling storage resources to be allocated dynamically based on demand. This means that storage can be provisioned more flexibly and used more efficiently, with the ability to adjust to changing workloads and business needs.

Centralizing storage in a SAN also simplifies storage management. Rather than managing individual storage devices attached to each server, administrators can manage all storage resources from a central location. This centralization allows for easier configuration, monitoring, and maintenance of storage systems. SAN management tools provide administrators with the ability to monitor the health and performance of the storage infrastructure, allocate storage dynamically, and implement policies such as backup and disaster recovery strategies. This streamlined approach to storage management saves time, reduces complexity, and allows administrators to focus on more strategic tasks.

Another significant benefit of SANs is the high performance they provide. SANs use high-speed network protocols, such as Fiber Channel or iSCSI, to enable fast data transfer between servers and storage devices. Fiber Channel, in particular, is designed specifically for storage networks, offering low-latency and high-throughput connections that ensure rapid data access. In large-scale enterprise environments, where data access speed is crucial for applications such as databases, data analytics, and virtualization, the high performance of SANs ensures that critical data can be retrieved and processed quickly. SANs also support advanced features such as data caching and tiered storage, which further enhance performance by prioritizing frequently accessed data and placing it on faster storage media, while less critical data is stored on slower devices.

Scalability is another key advantage of SANs for enterprise storage solutions. As businesses grow and their data storage needs increase, the ability to scale the storage infrastructure is critical. SANs are designed to be highly scalable, allowing organizations to add new storage devices, servers, and switches to the network as needed. The flexibility of SANs means that organizations can expand their storage capacity without disrupting existing operations. This is particularly important for enterprises that expect their data storage needs to grow over time, as it allows them to scale the infrastructure in a cost-effective manner, without needing to completely overhaul their storage environment. SANs also support non-disruptive upgrades, meaning that storage resources can be added or upgraded without causing downtime or affecting business operations.

The high availability and fault tolerance provided by SANs are crucial for enterprises that require constant access to their data. SANs are designed with redundancy built into their architecture, ensuring that storage resources remain available even in the event of hardware failures. This redundancy is typically achieved through the use of multiple paths between storage devices and servers, allowing for automatic failover if one path or device becomes unavailable. Additionally, SANs can be configured with redundant switches, HBAs, and storage devices to further enhance fault tolerance. In mission-critical environments, where downtime can result in significant financial loss or operational disruption, the ability to maintain continuous access to data is essential. SANs provide the high availability required for such environments, ensuring that data can always be accessed, even if part of the infrastructure fails.

Security is a major concern for enterprises, especially when it comes to protecting sensitive data. SANs provide a range of security features to help safeguard data, including zoning, authentication, and encryption. Zoning allows administrators to segment the SAN into logical groups, ensuring that only authorized devices can communicate with each other. This limits the risk of unauthorized access and ensures that sensitive data is isolated from other parts of the network. Authentication mechanisms, such as the Fiber Channel Security Protocol (FC-SP), provide an additional layer of security by verifying that only trusted devices can join the network. Encryption can also be applied to protect data as it travels across the SAN, ensuring that sensitive information remains secure even if intercepted. These security features make SANs an ideal solution for organizations that handle sensitive or regulated data.

Disaster recovery and data protection are also significantly improved with the use of SANs. By centralizing storage resources, SANs make it easier to implement backup, replication, and recovery strategies. Data replication can be set up between remote sites, ensuring that critical data is replicated in real-time or near real-time to a secondary location. This provides organizations with the ability to recover quickly in the event of a disaster, minimizing downtime and data loss. SANs can also integrate with backup solutions to ensure that data is regularly backed up and can be restored quickly if needed. The ability to quickly recover from a disaster is essential for maintaining business continuity, and SANs provide the tools necessary to implement comprehensive disaster recovery plans.

Another advantage of SANs for enterprise storage is the ability to integrate with other enterprise technologies, such as virtualization and cloud storage. SANs provide a high-performance, low-latency infrastructure that is ideal for supporting virtualized environments, where multiple virtual machines access shared storage resources. SANs enable the consolidation of storage resources, making it easier to manage virtualized workloads and ensure that data is available to virtual machines without delays. Additionally, SANs can be integrated with cloud storage solutions, enabling businesses to extend their storage infrastructure to the cloud and take advantage of the scalability and cost-efficiency of cloud storage while maintaining the performance and control provided by the SAN.

The benefits of SANs for enterprise storage solutions extend beyond performance and capacity. SANs also provide organizations with the flexibility to implement a wide range of storage configurations, such as tiered storage, snapshots, and cloning, that can further optimize storage utilization and performance. With tiered storage, organizations can store high-priority data on faster storage devices, while less critical data is stored on slower, more cost-effective devices. Snapshots and cloning allow for quick backups and the ability to create copies of data for testing or development purposes, without impacting the primary data set.

In summary, SANs offer numerous benefits for enterprise storage solutions, providing organizations with the tools necessary to optimize storage management, ensure high performance, and scale their infrastructure to meet growing data demands. With their ability to centralize storage resources, enhance data availability and security, and integrate with other technologies, SANs are an essential component of modern enterprise IT environments. As businesses continue to generate increasing amounts of data, SANs provide a flexible, reliable, and efficient way to manage and protect that data, ensuring that enterprises can continue to operate smoothly and maintain access to critical information.

Another important disaster recovery technique in SAN networks is the use of snapshot technology. Snapshots are point-in-time copies of the data that capture the state of the storage system at a particular moment. These snapshots can be used for backup purposes or to restore data to a specific point in time in the event of corruption or loss. SANs can be configured to automatically create snapshots at regular intervals, ensuring that a recent version of the data is always available for recovery. Snapshots are particularly useful in environments where rapid data recovery is required, as they provide a quick and efficient way to restore data without needing to perform a full restore from backup.

While traditional disaster recovery solutions focus on physical failures or disasters, it is also important to consider cyberattacks and ransomware, which pose significant risks to data security and availability. SANs provide several mechanisms to protect against such threats. One such mechanism is encryption, which ensures that data is protected both at rest and in transit. By encrypting data within the SAN, organizations can prevent unauthorized access in the event of a breach, ensuring that even if attackers gain access to the network, the data remains unreadable. Fiber Channel networks, with their dedicated infrastructure, also offer a level of isolation that makes them less susceptible to attacks compared to traditional IP-based networks, which are more vulnerable to remote cyberattacks. Additionally, SANs can be equipped with access control policies that restrict which devices and users can access specific storage resources, reducing the risk of unauthorized access.

The combination of data replication, backup strategies, failover mechanisms, snapshots, and encryption provides a multi-layered approach to disaster recovery and data protection in SAN networks. By ensuring that data is continuously protected, organizations can minimize the impact of system failures, natural disasters, or cyberattacks. Regular testing of disaster recovery plans is also critical to ensure that these mechanisms function correctly in real-world scenarios. Simulated disaster recovery tests allow IT teams to identify any gaps in their recovery process and ensure that the infrastructure is prepared to handle unexpected events.

Ultimately, the goal of disaster recovery and data protection in SAN networks is to ensure that data is always available when needed, regardless of the circumstances. SANs provide the foundation for achieving this goal by offering high availability, scalability, and reliability. With the right combination of replication, backup, failover, and encryption techniques, businesses can ensure that their data remains protected and accessible, even in the event of a disaster. By implementing a comprehensive disaster recovery strategy within the SAN, organizations can safeguard their critical assets and maintain business continuity in the face of unexpected events.

# Performance Monitoring and Troubleshooting in SAN Networks

Storage Area Networks (SANs) are integral to modern data center infrastructures, offering a high-performance, reliable, and scalable solution for managing large volumes of data. As businesses continue to grow, SANs become increasingly complex, connecting multiple servers, storage devices, and switches. The performance of a SAN directly impacts the efficiency of data access and storage operations, making performance monitoring and troubleshooting essential for maintaining the health of the network. By actively monitoring the performance of SAN components and addressing potential issues, administrators can ensure optimal network performance, reduce downtime, and maintain the availability of critical business data.

Performance monitoring in a SAN involves continuously assessing the health and functionality of the various components, including servers, storage devices, switches, and cabling. The goal is to track key performance metrics, identify any performance degradation, and prevent issues before they affect the overall system. One of the first steps in performance monitoring is identifying the key metrics that reflect the health and efficiency of the network. These metrics may include throughput, latency, error rates, disk I/O, and network utilization. By regularly gathering this data, administrators can establish baseline performance levels and quickly identify any deviations from normal operating conditions.

Throughput is one of the most important performance indicators in SAN networks. It measures the rate at which data is transferred across the network, typically in terms of megabytes or gigabytes per second. High throughput is essential for ensuring that data can be accessed quickly, particularly in high-demand environments such as virtualization, database operations, and real-time data processing. Monitoring throughput helps administrators ensure that the SAN is capable of handling the volume of data being generated by applications and users. If throughput drops below expected levels, it may indicate network congestion, bandwidth limitations, or faulty components that need attention.

Latency is another critical metric that measures the delay between sending a data request and receiving the corresponding response. Low latency is crucial for maintaining fast access to data, particularly in environments that require real-time data processing. High latency can result from network congestion, faulty cabling, or improperly configured hardware, leading to slower data access times and decreased overall performance. By monitoring latency, administrators can detect bottlenecks in the network and take corrective action to improve the responsiveness of the SAN.

Error rates are another key aspect of performance monitoring. Fiber Channel SANs use error-detection protocols, such as cyclic redundancy checks (CRC) and frame check sequences (FCS), to ensure that data is transmitted accurately across the network. If errors are detected, it may indicate issues with the cabling, switches, or storage devices. A high error rate can result in data corruption or transmission failures, so it is essential to monitor error counts regularly to prevent potential data integrity issues. An increase in error rates often signals the need for troubleshooting and corrective action, such as replacing faulty cables, switches, or devices.

Disk I/O performance is also a critical component of SAN monitoring. In a SAN, storage devices are shared by multiple servers, making it essential to ensure that each device is performing optimally. Monitoring disk I/O helps identify whether storage devices are underperforming or experiencing high levels of contention. Disk I/O bottlenecks can occur when too many requests are made to a particular disk or when a disk is unable to keep up with the volume of data being processed. By tracking disk I/O, administrators can identify performance issues and take steps to alleviate congestion, such as redistributing workloads, upgrading storage devices, or adding additional storage capacity.

Network utilization is another important metric to track in a SAN. SANs rely on high-speed networks, such as Fiber Channel or iSCSI, to transfer data between servers and storage devices. Monitoring network utilization helps administrators understand how much of the available bandwidth is being used and whether the network is being overloaded. If network utilization is consistently high, it may indicate the need for additional bandwidth or the reconfiguration of network resources to balance traffic more effectively. In large-scale SAN environments, network congestion can significantly impact performance, so proactive monitoring and management are necessary to prevent bottlenecks and ensure that the network operates efficiently.

Troubleshooting in SAN networks is a critical skill for administrators, as it enables them to diagnose and resolve issues quickly before they lead to significant disruptions. When performance degradation is detected, the first step in troubleshooting is to isolate the source of the issue. The process begins with examining the performance metrics to identify patterns and correlations. For example, if latency is increasing and throughput is decreasing, the issue may lie with a specific component, such as a switch or a storage device, rather than the entire network. Once the potential source of the problem is identified, administrators can focus their efforts on investigating that component further.

Common troubleshooting tasks include checking the physical connections between devices, verifying the health of switches, and inspecting storage devices for signs of failure. Fiber Channel switches, for example, can sometimes experience issues such as misconfigured zoning, firmware bugs, or hardware failures that affect their performance. In such cases, administrators may need to examine the switch logs, perform firmware upgrades, or reset the switch to restore functionality. Additionally, cabling issues, such as loose or damaged cables, can cause intermittent connectivity problems or degraded performance. Fiber optic cables, which are commonly used in SAN networks, require careful handling and maintenance to prevent signal degradation. Administrators must ensure that cables are properly connected, undamaged, and free from excessive bends or physical stress.

Another important aspect of troubleshooting involves checking the SAN's configuration settings. Misconfigured settings can often lead to performance issues, such as incorrect zoning, improper load balancing, or inefficient traffic routing. In such cases, administrators can review the SAN's configuration and make the necessary adjustments. For example, ensuring that multipathing is properly configured can prevent single points of failure and improve network reliability by providing alternate paths for data transmission. Ensuring that the storage devices are correctly integrated into the SAN and that access control policies are enforced can also help resolve issues related to data access and security.

In larger SAN environments, where hundreds or thousands of devices may be interconnected, the complexity of troubleshooting increases. To address this, administrators often rely on specialized SAN management software that provides real-time monitoring, diagnostics, and reporting capabilities. These tools allow administrators to track performance metrics, identify potential issues, and receive alerts when thresholds are exceeded. By leveraging these tools, administrators can proactively manage SAN performance and address problems before they escalate into more serious issues.

The performance of a SAN network is critical to the overall success of enterprise storage solutions. By implementing effective performance monitoring techniques and troubleshooting practices, administrators can ensure that the SAN operates at peak performance, delivering fast, reliable access to data. Monitoring key performance indicators such as throughput, latency, error rates, disk I/O, and network utilization allows administrators to detect potential issues early and take corrective action to prevent disruptions. Troubleshooting, when issues arise, requires a methodical approach to isolate and address the root cause of the problem, ensuring that the SAN remains operational and efficient. With the right tools and strategies in place, organizations can ensure that their SAN infrastructure continues to meet the performance requirements of modern applications and data-driven operations.

# Managing SAN Performance with Quality of Service (QoS)

In modern Storage Area Networks (SANs), ensuring high performance while meeting the demands of various applications and users is a complex challenge. As data storage needs continue to grow and become more varied, managing the performance of SANs has become increasingly important. One of the most effective methods for managing SAN performance and ensuring that critical applications receive the necessary resources is through the use of Quality of Service (QoS) mechanisms. QoS is a set of technologies and techniques used to control and prioritize data traffic, ensuring that network resources are allocated efficiently and according to the needs of the system. By implementing QoS in SANs, organizations can ensure that high-priority applications get the necessary bandwidth and that lower-priority tasks do not interfere with the performance of mission-critical processes.

The concept of QoS in SANs revolves around ensuring that data flows smoothly and efficiently between servers and storage devices, even when the network is under heavy load. One of the key objectives of QoS in a SAN environment is to prevent congestion and ensure that critical operations, such as database transactions or real-time processing, are not delayed by lower-priority tasks. In SANs, multiple servers and applications often share the same storage resources, which can lead to contention for bandwidth and storage access. Without proper management, this can result in degraded performance, slow data access times, and increased latency, which can have a significant impact on business operations.

One of the most important aspects of QoS in SANs is traffic prioritization. Traffic prioritization allows administrators to assign different levels of priority to various types of data traffic, ensuring that high-priority traffic, such as transactional or real-time data, receives the necessary bandwidth and resources. By setting priority levels, administrators can ensure that critical applications are not delayed by non-essential traffic. For example, in a SAN supporting both database applications and backup tasks, it would be crucial to prioritize database traffic over backup traffic. The database operations are time-sensitive, and any delay in accessing data could result in operational inefficiencies, while backup operations are less time-sensitive and can be scheduled for periods of lower network activity.

QoS is typically implemented using a combination of different techniques, including traffic shaping, congestion management, and bandwidth reservation. Traffic shaping involves controlling the flow of data to ensure that the network is not overloaded. It can be used to limit the amount of bandwidth consumed by less critical applications or users, preventing them from saturating the network and causing delays for higher-priority traffic. Congestion management techniques, such as flow control and buffer management, are used to ensure that the network does not become congested during periods of high traffic. These techniques manage how traffic is queued and transmitted through the network, ensuring that data is transmitted without interruption and that congestion does not occur. Bandwidth reservation, on the other hand, guarantees that a certain amount of bandwidth is always available for critical traffic. By reserving bandwidth for high-priority applications, administrators can ensure that performance remains consistent even during peak usage times.

Fiber Channel networks, which are commonly used in SANs, are inherently designed to support high-performance data transfer. However, without the implementation of QoS, the performance of Fiber Channel networks can be negatively impacted by network congestion, unpredictable traffic patterns, and competing demands for bandwidth. QoS provides the tools needed to manage these challenges by ensuring that the right traffic is prioritized and that resources are allocated efficiently. For example, Fiber Channel networks support the use of Traffic Classes (TCs), which define different priority levels for different types of traffic. By assigning different traffic classes to various data flows, administrators can ensure that critical applications are always given the necessary resources to function optimally.

One of the challenges of managing SAN performance with QoS is the complexity of configuring and tuning the system. A SAN typically consists of multiple components, including servers, storage devices, switches, and networking equipment, all of which need to be properly configured to work together efficiently. QoS settings must be applied at each layer of the network to ensure that traffic is prioritized correctly and that resources are allocated based on the requirements of each application. This can involve configuring switches to recognize and prioritize different types of traffic, setting up storage devices to support high-priority data access, and configuring servers to handle high-priority requests first. Moreover, the dynamic nature of SANs, where workloads can shift and change over time, means that administrators must continually monitor and adjust QoS settings to maintain optimal performance.

Monitoring QoS metrics is another critical aspect of managing SAN performance. By regularly tracking performance indicators such as throughput, latency, and error rates, administrators can identify potential issues before they impact the network. QoS monitoring tools can provide real-time visibility into how network resources are being utilized, allowing administrators to make adjustments as necessary. For instance, if a particular application is consuming more bandwidth than expected, administrators can use QoS tools to adjust its priority level or apply traffic shaping to ensure that it does not interfere with other critical applications. By continuously monitoring QoS metrics, administrators can ensure that the network is always performing at its best, even as demand fluctuates.

The benefits of QoS in SANs extend beyond just performance improvement. By implementing QoS, organizations can ensure that storage resources are utilized efficiently, which helps reduce operational costs. Instead of over-provisioning storage to account for peak traffic demands, QoS allows administrators to allocate storage resources dynamically based on actual usage patterns. This enables businesses to maximize the value of their storage infrastructure, avoiding the need to purchase unnecessary additional storage capacity. Moreover, QoS can help optimize energy consumption in data centers by ensuring that the network operates efficiently and that resources are allocated based on demand.

In addition to improving performance and resource utilization, QoS also plays a significant role in ensuring the reliability and availability of data in SANs. By prioritizing critical traffic and guaranteeing bandwidth for high-priority applications, QoS helps ensure that mission-critical data can always be accessed quickly and without delay. This is particularly important in industries such as healthcare, finance, and e-commerce, where even small delays in data access can have significant consequences. By implementing QoS, organizations can reduce the risk of data access delays and ensure that their SANs meet the performance and reliability requirements of their most important applications.

Managing SAN performance with QoS requires a comprehensive approach that involves understanding the needs of different applications, configuring the network to support those needs, and continuously monitoring performance to ensure that resources are allocated efficiently. By leveraging QoS technologies and techniques, administrators can ensure that SANs deliver the performance, scalability, and reliability required to support modern business applications. As data volumes continue to grow and business operations become increasingly dependent on fast and reliable access to storage resources, the importance of QoS in SANs will only continue to grow.

# Fiber Channel Network Management Protocols

Fiber Channel (FC) networks have become a cornerstone for enterprise storage solutions due to their high-speed, low-latency communication capabilities and reliability. As businesses continue to generate and process vast amounts of data, managing these networks efficiently becomes increasingly important. Network management in Fiber Channel environments involves not only monitoring the physical and logical components of the network but also ensuring that they function optimally to support demanding workloads. Effective management protocols are essential for maintaining network health, troubleshooting issues, ensuring security, and providing a scalable infrastructure for future growth. The Fiber Channel network management protocols play a critical role in ensuring the proper functioning of these networks, from basic connectivity to advanced troubleshooting and optimization.

Fiber Channel networks are designed to interconnect storage devices and servers within a storage area network (SAN). These networks require robust management protocols to monitor network performance, maintain the configuration of devices, and ensure that data is transferred reliably. Several key protocols are used to manage and control Fiber Channel networks, including the Fiber Channel Management Protocol (FC-MAN), the Fabric OS (FOS), Simple Network Management Protocol (SNMP), and the Link Control Protocol (LCP), among others. Each of these protocols serves a different function but collectively ensures the effective operation of a Fiber Channel network.

The Fiber Channel Management Protocol (FC-MAN) is a standard protocol designed to manage the entire Fiber Channel fabric. It provides a framework for managing all aspects of the network, including devices, links, and fabric topology. The FC-MAN protocol allows administrators to view the topology of the Fiber Channel network and track the status and health of devices within the fabric. Through FC-MAN, administrators can configure, monitor, and troubleshoot the network, ensuring that devices are connected properly and that communication between devices remains optimal. The protocol provides a way to identify issues such as malfunctioning switches, faulty cables, or other problems that could affect the network's performance.

FC-MAN is particularly useful in large-scale SAN environments, where managing individual devices and connections manually can become difficult. By utilizing FC-MAN, administrators can automate many of the configuration tasks and simplify the management of large, complex networks. FC-MAN is typically implemented in conjunction with other management protocols, such as SNMP, to provide a comprehensive management solution for Fiber Channel networks. The use of FC-MAN helps ensure that the network is operating efficiently and that any issues are detected early, minimizing downtime and ensuring high availability.

Fabric OS (FOS) is another key management protocol used in Fiber Channel networks. FOS is an operating system used by Fiber Channel switches and is designed to manage the fabric within a SAN. It provides a set of services for fabric management, including the ability to configure switches, monitor performance, and maintain fault tolerance across the fabric. FOS includes tools that allow administrators to manage zoning, security, and redundancy within the SAN fabric. Zoning, for example, is a critical feature of FOS that allows administrators to define logical groups of devices within the SAN, ensuring that only authorized devices can communicate with each other. This adds an extra layer of security and performance optimization to the network.

FOS is also essential for managing the flow of traffic between devices. By using FOS, administrators can optimize the path selection for data traffic, ensuring that data is transmitted via the fastest and most efficient route within the SAN. FOS also includes features for monitoring the health of switches and other devices in the fabric. For example, it can provide alerts when devices fail or experience performance degradation, allowing administrators to take corrective action before the issue affects the broader network. The protocol's ability to manage fabric-level redundancy, load balancing, and fault tolerance ensures that the SAN remains highly available and resilient, even in the face of hardware failures.

Simple Network Management Protocol (SNMP) is widely used in IP-based networks for monitoring and managing devices. It is also applied in Fiber Channel networks to monitor the status of various devices and components. SNMP is a simple yet powerful protocol that allows administrators to remotely manage devices, collect performance data, and receive notifications about network events. In Fiber Channel networks, SNMP can be used to monitor the status of Fiber Channel switches, HBAs (Host Bus Adapters), storage devices, and other network components. SNMP provides a standardized way to query devices for information such as port status, traffic statistics, and error rates, making it a valuable tool for diagnosing issues and maintaining optimal network performance.

SNMP works by using a set of management information bases (MIBs), which are standardized databases that define the variables that can be monitored on a device. Each device in a Fiber Channel network that supports SNMP will have its own MIB, which allows administrators to retrieve data about the device's status and health. SNMP provides both polling and alerting capabilities, enabling administrators to actively monitor devices or be notified automatically when an issue occurs. By integrating SNMP with other management tools, administrators can create a comprehensive monitoring system that provides real-time insights into the performance and health of the entire SAN.

The Link Control Protocol (LCP) is another key protocol used in Fiber Channel networks, particularly for managing the link between devices. LCP ensures that the physical links between Fiber Channel devices are functioning correctly and that the connection between switches, servers, and storage devices is stable. It is used to detect and correct errors that may occur during data transmission. LCP also plays a role in managing the link initialization process, ensuring that devices can establish reliable communication before transferring data. By maintaining the integrity of the link layer, LCP ensures that data is transmitted without corruption or loss, which is critical in high-performance storage environments where data integrity is paramount.

Together, these management protocols provide a comprehensive framework for managing Fiber Channel networks, from the physical link layer all the way to the higher-level fabric management and monitoring of devices. They enable administrators to maintain the health and performance of the network, troubleshoot issues, and ensure that the SAN operates optimally. Effective network management is essential for minimizing downtime, preventing data loss, and ensuring that storage resources are used efficiently.

In a large SAN environment, where hundreds or thousands of devices may be connected, the role of management protocols becomes even more important. Automation of configuration, monitoring, and troubleshooting tasks is crucial for maintaining a high level of performance and availability. Advanced management systems that integrate with Fiber Channel protocols can provide administrators with a single interface to view and manage the entire SAN infrastructure. By leveraging these management protocols, organizations can ensure that their Fiber Channel networks remain reliable, efficient, and scalable as their storage needs grow and evolve.

Fiber Channel network management protocols are fundamental to maintaining a high-performing, reliable, and secure storage infrastructure. By using protocols such as FC-MAN, FOS, SNMP, and

LCP, administrators can effectively manage, monitor, and troubleshoot their SANs, ensuring that critical data is always available and that performance remains optimal. These protocols enable organizations to scale their storage environments, integrate new devices, and maintain the health of their network, providing the necessary tools to support modern data-driven business operations.

# Storage Resource Management in SAN

Storage Resource Management (SRM) in Storage Area Networks (SANs) is a critical component for ensuring efficient, reliable, and scalable data storage. SANs provide centralized storage resources that are shared across multiple servers, creating a unified infrastructure for data storage, management, and access. With the increasing volume and complexity of data, effective storage management becomes essential to optimize performance, prevent downtime, and ensure that storage resources are used efficiently. SRM is the process of planning, monitoring, and maintaining the storage infrastructure within a SAN, ensuring that storage resources are allocated appropriately, performance remains optimal, and costs are minimized.

At the heart of SRM is the ability to allocate storage resources dynamically based on the needs of different applications and users. In a SAN, storage resources are pooled together, allowing administrators to manage and allocate storage capacity in a more flexible and efficient manner. One of the primary goals of SRM is to ensure that the right amount of storage is available to meet the needs of various workloads while preventing over-provisioning or under-utilization. By centrally managing the storage resources, administrators can allocate storage to different servers or applications as needed, ensuring that resources are used optimally. This dynamic allocation helps to prevent storage bottlenecks and ensures that the SAN infrastructure can scale as business needs evolve.

One of the key features of SRM is the ability to monitor and track storage usage across the SAN. This monitoring process involves continuously collecting data about the performance of storage devices, such as disk arrays, and tracking how much storage is being used by different servers, applications, and users. By collecting this data, administrators can gain visibility into storage utilization, identify under-utilized storage devices, and optimize the distribution of storage resources. This allows for more efficient use of storage capacity, as storage can be reallocated to areas where it is needed most. Monitoring also helps to identify potential issues before they impact performance, such as a storage device approaching its capacity limits or performance degradation due to heavy usage.

In addition to monitoring storage usage, SRM tools can provide detailed insights into the performance of the SAN infrastructure. These tools can track key performance indicators (KPIs), such as throughput, latency, and I/O performance, across the SAN. By measuring these metrics, administrators can identify performance bottlenecks and take corrective actions to improve overall performance. For example, if one storage device is experiencing high latency or slow data access speeds, it can be flagged for further investigation or replacement. By closely monitoring performance and addressing any issues, administrators can ensure that the SAN continues to operate at peak efficiency.

Another important aspect of SRM in SANs is the management of storage policies. Policies are used to define how storage resources are allocated, how data is protected, and how performance is optimized across the network. SRM tools allow administrators to configure policies that govern how storage is used based on factors such as the criticality of the application, the amount of available storage, and the performance requirements. For example, administrators can implement Quality of Service (QoS) policies to prioritize certain types of traffic or allocate more storage resources to high-priority applications. These policies help to ensure that critical workloads receive the necessary resources, while non-critical tasks are allocated less capacity.

Data protection and backup are also key elements of SRM in SANs. Protecting data against loss due to hardware failures, corruption, or disasters is essential in any storage environment. In SANs, data protection strategies can be implemented at various levels, including device-level replication, volume-level snapshots, and host-level backups. SRM tools help administrators manage these protection mechanisms by automating backup processes, scheduling data replication, and ensuring that data is consistently protected. With SAN-based replication, data can be mirrored to remote storage devices or off-site locations, providing redundancy and ensuring that data is recoverable in the event of a disaster. Snapshots allow administrators to take point-in-time copies of data, making it easy to recover from accidental deletion or corruption. By effectively managing these data protection strategies, SRM helps to ensure that business-critical data is safe and readily available.

Capacity planning is another crucial aspect of SRM in SANs. As data volumes continue to grow, it is important to anticipate future storage needs and plan accordingly. SRM tools help administrators forecast storage requirements by analyzing historical data usage patterns and predicting future growth. This allows organizations to proactively add storage capacity before it becomes a bottleneck, avoiding performance degradation or system outages. Capacity planning also involves optimizing the use of existing storage resources, ensuring that storage is allocated efficiently and that unused or under-utilized storage is reclaimed. By planning for future growth and optimizing current resources, SRM helps organizations avoid costly and disruptive storage expansions.

SRM also plays a vital role in ensuring compliance with data management policies and regulatory requirements. Many industries, such as healthcare, finance, and government, are subject to strict regulations regarding data retention, security, and access. SRM tools can help organizations enforce these regulations by providing audit trails, access control, and data retention policies. These tools can track who accessed the data, when it was accessed, and any modifications made, ensuring that the organization can meet compliance requirements and avoid penalties. Data retention policies can also be set to ensure that data is stored for the required period and securely deleted when no longer needed, preventing unauthorized access and ensuring the privacy of sensitive data.

As SANs continue to evolve and grow in complexity, automation becomes an increasingly important part of SRM. Automated tools can simplify many of the tasks associated with storage management, such as provisioning new storage devices, managing backups, and optimizing resource allocation. Automation reduces the need for manual intervention, minimizes the risk of human error, and ensures that tasks are performed consistently and on schedule. For example, automated provisioning can be used to quickly allocate storage to new servers or applications, ensuring that resources are available when needed without delays. Automated monitoring can detect issues in real-time and trigger alerts or corrective actions before problems escalate.

Integration with other IT management tools is also an important aspect of SRM. Many organizations use various tools for managing other aspects of their IT infrastructure, such as networking, virtualization, and security. By integrating SRM tools with these other management systems, administrators can gain a more comprehensive view of the entire infrastructure. This integration allows for better coordination between storage, compute, and network resources, enabling more efficient management of the overall IT environment. For example, when a new virtual machine is provisioned, the SRM tool can automatically allocate the appropriate amount of storage to support the VM, ensuring that it has the necessary resources for optimal performance.

Effective storage resource management in SANs is crucial for ensuring that organizations can meet the growing demands for data storage and access. By dynamically allocating resources, monitoring performance, and implementing data protection strategies, administrators can ensure that their SANs are running efficiently and that data is always available when needed. SRM tools provide the necessary visibility and control to manage storage resources effectively, allowing organizations to optimize their storage infrastructure and support the needs of modern applications. As the complexity and scale of data storage continue to increase, SRM will remain a critical element in maintaining the reliability, performance, and security of SAN environments.

# SAN Design Principles: Planning and Implementation

Designing and implementing a Storage Area Network (SAN) requires careful planning and a deep understanding of the network's requirements, performance needs, and scalability. The complexity and scale of SANs, which are integral to enterprise-level data storage, make it essential to approach the design with a structured methodology. From selecting the right hardware components to determining the best network topology, each aspect of SAN design plays a crucial role in ensuring that the network functions efficiently, securely, and reliably. A well-designed SAN not only meets the current storage needs of an organization but also supports future growth and adapts to changing business demands.

The first step in planning a SAN design is to assess the storage needs of the organization. This involves understanding the types of data that need to be stored, how that data will be accessed, and the performance requirements of the applications using the SAN. For instance, high-performance applications like databases and real-time analytics demand low-latency access to data, while backup and archival systems may have less stringent performance requirements but require high capacity and reliability. A thorough analysis of these factors helps ensure that the right mix of storage devices and networking components is selected to meet both the current and future needs of the organization.

Once the storage requirements are understood, the next step is to select the appropriate storage devices and determine how they will be integrated into the SAN. The choice of storage devices, whether disk arrays, solid-state drives (SSDs), or tape libraries, will depend on the specific needs of the organization. Disk arrays are typically used for high-capacity, high-performance storage, while SSDs offer faster data access times and are well-suited for performance-sensitive applications. Tape libraries, though less common in modern SANs, are still used for long-term archival and backup purposes. The integration of these devices into the SAN must be carefully planned to ensure that they work seamlessly with the rest of the infrastructure. This includes selecting appropriate interfaces, such as Fiber Channel or iSCSI, and configuring them to optimize performance and reliability.

The design of the SAN network topology is another critical consideration in the planning process. The network topology determines how devices, servers, and switches are connected and how data flows across the network. In a typical SAN, a switched fabric topology is used, where multiple switches interconnect servers and storage devices, creating a robust and scalable network. This topology offers numerous advantages, including redundancy, load balancing, and high availability. However, the design must take into account factors such as the number of devices to be connected, the distance between them, and the required bandwidth. A well-designed topology ensures that data flows efficiently between devices and that the network can handle the volume of data being transmitted without becoming congested.

Redundancy is a key principle in SAN design, particularly for mission-critical applications. In environments where downtime is unacceptable, it is essential to ensure that the SAN can continue to function even in the event of hardware failure. Redundancy is typically implemented by having multiple paths between devices, so if one path fails, traffic can be rerouted through an alternate path. This can be achieved using technologies such as multipathing and fabric redundancy. Multipathing provides multiple data paths between servers and storage devices, while fabric redundancy involves using multiple switches to create a fault-tolerant network. By implementing these redundancy techniques, the SAN can maintain high availability and minimize the risk of data loss or downtime.

Scalability is another important factor in SAN design. As the volume of data grows and business needs evolve, the SAN must be able to scale to accommodate increased storage capacity and additional devices. A well-designed SAN allows for easy expansion by adding new storage devices, switches, or servers without disrupting existing operations. Scalability can be achieved by using modular components, such as scalable switches and storage arrays, which can be easily expanded as the network grows. It is also important to plan for future bandwidth requirements to ensure that the network can handle the increased traffic as more devices and applications are added to the SAN.

Security is an essential consideration in the design of a SAN, particularly when sensitive data is being stored and transmitted. A SAN must be secured against unauthorized access, data breaches, and cyber threats. One of the primary methods of securing a SAN is through zoning, which allows administrators to define logical groups of devices within the SAN and control which devices can communicate with each other. By implementing zoning, organizations can isolate sensitive data and ensure that only authorized devices have access to it. Other security measures, such as encryption, authentication, and access control, can also be used to further protect data within the SAN. Encryption ensures that data is unreadable if intercepted, while authentication verifies the identity of devices attempting to connect to the SAN.

Once the design and hardware selections are finalized, the implementation phase begins. During this phase, the components are physically installed, configured, and tested. It is important to follow best practices during the installation process to ensure that all components are properly connected and configured. This includes ensuring that switches are correctly configured with the appropriate zoning settings, that devices are properly connected to the network, and that storage devices are integrated into the SAN fabric. The installation process should also include testing to verify that the SAN is operating as expected, with all components functioning correctly and data being transmitted efficiently.

One key element of the implementation phase is performance testing. It is crucial to ensure that the SAN meets the required performance standards, such as throughput, latency, and I/O operations per second (IOPS). Performance testing allows administrators to identify any potential bottlenecks in the network and make adjustments as necessary. This may involve optimizing the network topology, upgrading hardware, or fine-tuning the configuration of storage devices. It is also important to ensure that the SAN is configured to handle peak workloads and that the network is capable of scaling as business needs grow.

Once the SAN is up and running, ongoing management and monitoring are essential for maintaining optimal performance and addressing any issues that may arise. SAN management involves monitoring key metrics, such as storage utilization, performance, and error rates, to ensure that the network continues to meet the needs of the organization. Management tools can be used to track device health, monitor traffic, and identify potential issues before they affect performance. Regular maintenance tasks, such as firmware updates, hardware upgrades, and configuration adjustments, should also be scheduled to ensure that the SAN remains secure and efficient.

The design and implementation of a SAN are ongoing processes that require careful attention to detail, from the initial planning stages to the ongoing maintenance and optimization. A well-designed SAN can provide an organization with a reliable, scalable, and high-performance storage solution that meets its current and future data storage needs. By carefully considering factors such as hardware selection, network topology, redundancy, scalability, and security, administrators can build a SAN that delivers the performance and reliability required for mission-critical applications. Through proactive management and regular monitoring, the SAN can continue to support the growing demands of the business, ensuring that data is always available and accessible when needed.

# Managing Fiber Channel with SAN Management Software

Fiber Channel (FC) networks are integral to modern storage infrastructures, providing high-speed, low-latency communication between servers, storage devices, and other components in a Storage Area Network (SAN). As businesses generate increasing amounts of data, effectively managing the performance, scalability, and reliability of these networks becomes increasingly complex. SAN management software plays a vital role in helping administrators configure, monitor, and optimize Fiber Channel networks. By leveraging the capabilities of SAN management software, organizations can ensure their FC networks perform efficiently, meet business demands, and maintain high availability and data integrity.

The primary function of SAN management software is to provide a centralized interface for administrators to configure, manage, and monitor their Fiber Channel infrastructure. These tools are designed to simplify the complex tasks involved in managing SANs, offering features such as device discovery, network topology visualization, performance monitoring, zoning configuration, and troubleshooting. Managing a SAN without such software would involve manually configuring each switch, server, and storage device, which can be time-consuming and prone to errors. SAN management software automates many of these tasks, making it easier for administrators to ensure the health and performance of the network.

One of the most important features of SAN management software is its ability to visualize and map the network topology. The topology of a Fiber Channel SAN defines how the various devices, including servers, switches, and storage arrays, are interconnected. Understanding the network topology is essential for managing traffic, configuring zoning, and troubleshooting. SAN management software automatically discovers devices in the network and creates a graphical map that displays how devices are connected. This map allows administrators to quickly identify the physical and logical layout of the network and determine if there are any issues, such as incorrect connections or misconfigured devices. Visualization tools help administrators gain insight into the network's structure and make informed decisions about how to optimize performance or address issues.

In addition to topology mapping, SAN management software allows administrators to configure zoning, a key element in Fiber Channel SANs. Zoning is the process of dividing the SAN into logical segments, ensuring that only authorized devices can communicate with each other. By isolating devices into different zones, administrators can improve security, manage traffic, and prevent unauthorized access to sensitive data. SAN management software simplifies the process of creating and managing zones, providing administrators with an intuitive interface to define and configure zones based on physical ports or World Wide Names (WWNs). Zoning is essential for maintaining the security and performance of the SAN, and the use of SAN management software makes this task more efficient and less error-prone.

Another important function of SAN management software is performance monitoring. Fiber Channel networks are designed for high-speed, low-latency communication, but performance can degrade if there are issues in the network, such as congestion, faulty hardware, or configuration errors. SAN management software continuously monitors key performance metrics, including throughput, latency, error rates, and IOPS (Input/Output Operations Per Second), and provides real-time insights into the health of the network. Performance monitoring allows administrators to track network usage patterns, identify bottlenecks, and make adjustments to optimize performance. For example, if a storage device is experiencing high latency or a network path is congested, administrators can use the software to quickly identify the issue and take corrective action.

In addition to monitoring performance, SAN management software helps with troubleshooting and fault detection. Identifying and resolving issues in a Fiber Channel network can be complex due to the many interconnected components and the high-speed nature of the communication. SAN management software provides diagnostic tools that allow administrators to identify the source of a problem quickly. These tools may include alerts for hardware failures, performance degradation, or configuration mismatches, as well as the ability to examine device logs and error messages. In the event of a failure, SAN management software can help administrators pinpoint the location of the problem, whether it's a switch, cable, server, or storage device. By streamlining the troubleshooting process, SAN management software reduces downtime and minimizes the impact of issues on business operations.

Scalability is another critical consideration when managing a Fiber Channel network. As organizations grow and their storage needs increase, SANs must be able to scale to accommodate additional devices, servers, and storage arrays. SAN management software simplifies the process of scaling the network by allowing administrators to easily add new devices and configure them to integrate seamlessly with the existing infrastructure. With proper management tools, administrators can monitor the impact of adding new devices on network performance and ensure that the additional resources are properly allocated. This level of scalability is essential for supporting the growth of businesses and ensuring that their storage infrastructure remains flexible and capable of handling increased workloads.

Security is a fundamental aspect of managing Fiber Channel networks, especially in environments where sensitive data is being transmitted. SAN management software helps enforce security policies by providing features such as access control, authentication, and encryption. By using these tools, administrators can ensure that only authorized devices and users can access storage resources, reducing the risk of unauthorized access or data breaches. For instance, SAN management software allows administrators to define user roles and permissions, ensuring that individuals can only access the parts of the network they are authorized to use. Additionally, encryption can be enabled within the software to protect data both at rest and in transit, ensuring that sensitive information is secure throughout its lifecycle.

Automation is another key benefit of SAN management software. By automating routine tasks such as provisioning storage, configuring devices, and applying updates, administrators can reduce the administrative burden and minimize the risk of human error. Automation also allows for faster deployment of new storage resources, enabling organizations to scale their infrastructure quickly in response to changing business needs. For example, when provisioning new storage for a server, SAN management software can automatically allocate the appropriate amount of storage from the pool, configure the necessary zoning, and apply any relevant performance or security policies. This automation reduces the time spent on manual tasks and ensures that storage is provisioned consistently and correctly.

Integration with other IT management tools is another advantage of SAN management software. Many organizations use various tools to manage different aspects of their IT infrastructure, such as network management, virtualization, and backup. SAN management software can often integrate with these other tools, providing administrators with a unified view of the entire IT environment. This integration allows for better coordination between different components, ensuring that storage resources are aligned with network, compute, and application requirements. For example, SAN management software can be integrated with virtualization platforms to automatically allocate storage to virtual machines based on their needs, ensuring that virtualized environments have the necessary storage capacity to function effectively.

The role of SAN management software in managing Fiber Channel networks is crucial for ensuring that these high-performance infrastructures remain secure, reliable, and efficient. By providing tools for monitoring performance, configuring devices, automating tasks, and troubleshooting issues, SAN management software simplifies the complexities of managing Fiber Channel networks and ensures that organizations can meet their data storage needs. With the increasing demand for data and the growing complexity of storage environments, SAN management software is an essential tool for maintaining the health and performance of Fiber Channel networks and ensuring that they continue to meet the needs of modern businesses.

# Fault Isolation and Diagnosis in Fiber Channel Networks

Fiber Channel networks are a critical component of modern enterprise storage infrastructures, providing fast, reliable, and high-performance data transmission between servers, storage devices, and other network components. Due to their complexity and the importance of data reliability, ensuring that these networks remain operational and free from faults is essential for maintaining business continuity. However, like any advanced network, Fiber Channel systems are susceptible to faults, which can arise from a variety of sources, including hardware failures, configuration errors, network congestion, and connectivity issues. Effectively isolating and diagnosing faults in these networks is vital for ensuring that issues are quickly identified and resolved, minimizing downtime and preventing disruptions to critical services.

Fault isolation and diagnosis in Fiber Channel networks require a systematic approach that involves monitoring, troubleshooting, and understanding the intricate interactions between network components. The first step in isolating faults is to understand the network topology and the different components involved. In a typical Fiber Channel network, devices such as switches, storage arrays, host

101

bus adapters (HBAs), and cables work together to facilitate communication. Each of these components plays a vital role in ensuring smooth data transfer, and understanding their interdependencies is crucial for diagnosing any faults that may arise. When a fault occurs, the first task is to determine which component or combination of components is responsible for the issue, and this is where monitoring tools and diagnostic methods become essential.

One of the primary challenges in Fiber Channel networks is identifying the root cause of a problem. Unlike traditional IP networks, where troubleshooting often focuses on packet-level issues, Fiber Channel networks operate on a different layer, with specific protocols for error detection, link management, and communication between devices. Common faults in Fiber Channel networks can include issues with link connectivity, misconfigurations, or hardware failures, all of which can disrupt the flow of data and affect network performance. Detecting these faults requires a comprehensive approach that involves both physical and logical diagnostic techniques.

Network management software is one of the most valuable tools for fault isolation in Fiber Channel networks. These tools allow administrators to monitor the health of the entire network and provide real-time visibility into key metrics such as throughput, latency, error rates, and device status. By analyzing this data, administrators can identify potential issues early, before they escalate into larger problems. Network management tools can provide alerts when thresholds for specific metrics are exceeded, such as when a storage device or switch is operating at suboptimal performance or when error rates rise above acceptable levels. This proactive monitoring enables administrators to address problems before they impact critical business operations, allowing for faster response times and minimizing the likelihood of prolonged network downtime.

Once a fault is detected, the next step is fault isolation, which involves narrowing down the source of the problem. Fault isolation in Fiber Channel networks often begins with identifying whether the issue is related to the physical layer, the link layer, or the protocol layer. Physical layer issues may involve damaged cables, faulty HBAs, or defective ports, while link layer issues may arise from misconfigurations in the switches or issues with the flow control mechanisms. Protocol layer issues can stem from problems with the Fiber Channel protocol itself, such as incorrect framing, packet loss, or checksum mismatches. By isolating the layer where the fault originates, administrators can more effectively target the root cause and take appropriate corrective action.

In cases where the fault is related to the physical layer, administrators may need to perform tests to verify the integrity of cables, connectors, and other physical components. Fiber optic cables, which are commonly used in Fiber Channel networks, can suffer from wear and tear, leading to poor signal quality or intermittent connectivity. Fiber optic connectors can also become dirty or damaged, leading to signal loss or degradation. Tools such as optical time-domain reflectometers (OTDRs) can be used to test the integrity of fiber optic cables and locate breaks, bends, or other issues that may affect the network. Similarly, testing the HBAs and ports can help determine if the hardware is functioning properly. By checking for error messages, status indicators, or conducting loopback tests, administrators can confirm whether the hardware is causing the issue.

When a fault is detected at the link or protocol layer, the next step is to investigate the configuration settings of the switches, zoning configurations, and other network parameters. Misconfigured zoning, for example, can cause devices within the SAN to be unable to communicate with each other, leading to network failures. Zoning errors can be difficult to detect, especially in large-scale networks, where hundreds or thousands of devices are connected. SAN management software can be used to review zoning configurations, ensuring that devices are correctly grouped and that only authorized devices can access specific storage resources. Misconfigurations in the flow control mechanisms of switches or the fabric can also lead to congestion or poor network performance. Diagnosing such issues may involve checking the settings for buffer credits, flow control settings, or link speeds to ensure that data is flowing efficiently across the network.

In situations where more complex faults arise, such as protocol-related issues, administrators must look deeper into the behavior of the Fiber Channel protocol itself. Fiber Channel networks use specific communication protocols that define how data is transmitted and verified between devices. Issues such as incorrect frame formats, failed handshakes, or CRC (Cyclic Redundancy Check) mismatches can cause data transmission failures and impact network performance. Diagnostic tools built into SAN management software can provide detailed information about frame transmissions, errors, and protocol mismatches, helping administrators to identify where the communication breakdown occurs.

Once the fault is isolated and diagnosed, the next step is remediation, which involves taking corrective action to restore network performance. Remediation can range from replacing faulty hardware components, such as switches, cables, or HBAs, to adjusting configuration settings, such as increasing buffer credits or reconfiguring zoning. For physical layer issues, administrators may need to replace or repair cables, connectors, or other hardware, while link layer issues may require adjustments to switch configurations or changes in network topology. In cases where protocol errors are identified, firmware or software updates may be required to address bugs or incompatibilities that are affecting communication. By addressing the root cause of the problem, administrators can restore the network to optimal performance and prevent future issues from arising.

Effective fault isolation and diagnosis in Fiber Channel networks are essential for maintaining the reliability, availability, and performance of a SAN. Given the critical role that these networks play in supporting data storage and business operations, quickly identifying and addressing faults is key to preventing downtime and ensuring that storage resources are always available when needed. By utilizing monitoring tools, diagnostic procedures, and remediation techniques, administrators can keep Fiber Channel networks running smoothly and meet the ever-growing demands of modern enterprise environments.

# Fiber Channel Over IP (FCIP) and WAN Connectivity

Fiber Channel over IP (FCIP) is an innovative technology that allows organizations to extend their Storage Area Networks (SANs) across wide geographical areas, enabling long-distance data transfer over existing IP-based networks such as the internet or corporate wide-area networks (WANs). By encapsulating Fiber Channel frames into IP packets, FCIP makes it possible to transmit storage traffic over a more cost-effective and widely available network infrastructure compared to traditional Fiber Channel-based networks. This capability is especially valuable for businesses with distributed data centers, remote offices, or global operations, as it facilitates the replication of critical data and provides disaster recovery capabilities over vast distances.

The primary advantage of FCIP is its ability to leverage existing IP-based WAN infrastructures for high-performance storage traffic. Typically, Fiber Channel networks require dedicated, high-bandwidth, low-latency connections, such as those provided by Fiber Channel over dedicated fiber optic links. These dedicated connections are expensive and can be difficult to scale. However, FCIP enables the use of IP-based networks, which are more affordable, more readily available, and easier to scale. By using FCIP, organizations can extend their SANs to remote locations without the need to invest in specialized, proprietary networks, significantly reducing the overall cost of SAN deployments and enhancing flexibility.

One of the key features of FCIP is the encapsulation of Fiber Channel frames into IP packets. Fiber Channel frames, which carry storage traffic in a SAN, are not natively compatible with IP networks. To address this, FCIP uses a tunneling technique where Fiber Channel frames are encapsulated into standard IP packets for transmission across the WAN. At the receiving end, the encapsulated packets are de-encapsulated and converted back into Fiber Channel frames. This process allows SANs to operate across IP networks without disrupting the underlying Fiber Channel protocol, preserving the high performance and low latency that Fiber Channel is known for while leveraging the broader reach and lower cost of IP infrastructure.

One of the challenges in using FCIP over WANs is ensuring that the storage traffic is transmitted reliably and efficiently, especially when crossing public or private IP networks. WANs introduce several factors that can impact performance, such as network congestion, latency, packet loss, and bandwidth limitations. To mitigate these challenges, FCIP incorporates several techniques to optimize data transfer across WANs. Compression, for instance, reduces the amount of data that needs to be transmitted, which helps to maximize bandwidth utilization. Additionally, FCIP uses mechanisms such as error correction and flow control to ensure that data is transmitted accurately and reliably. These techniques are essential for ensuring that SAN traffic remains fast and reliable, even over long distances or in environments with fluctuating network conditions.

Latency is another key consideration when implementing FCIP over WANs. Fiber Channel networks are designed to provide low-latency communication, which is crucial for many storage applications that require near-instantaneous data access. However, when SAN traffic is extended over WANs, latency can increase due to the longer distances the data must travel and the additional processing required for encapsulation and de-encapsulation. To address this, FCIP solutions often include features like traffic prioritization and Quality of Service (QoS) mechanisms to ensure that storage traffic is given higher priority over less time-sensitive traffic. This ensures that SAN performance is not compromised, even in congested or high-latency environments.

One of the most common use cases for FCIP is in disaster recovery and data replication. With FCIP, organizations can replicate data across geographically dispersed data centers, ensuring that data is protected and available even in the event of a site failure. By extending the SAN to remote locations via FCIP, businesses can create a more resilient IT infrastructure that is better equipped to handle outages, natural disasters, or other disruptions. Data replication over FCIP can be configured for synchronous or asynchronous modes, depending on the organization's requirements for data consistency and recovery time objectives (RTO). Synchronous replication ensures that data is mirrored in real-time, providing the highest level of data protection, while asynchronous replication allows for a slight delay between the source and destination, which can be more suitable for environments where a small amount of data loss is acceptable.

FCIP also plays a significant role in enabling storage consolidation for distributed environments. Organizations that operate multiple data centers across different geographic locations often struggle with managing and scaling their storage infrastructure. By using FCIP, businesses can consolidate storage resources into a single, centrally managed SAN, which can be accessed from remote sites across the WAN. This reduces the complexity and cost associated with maintaining multiple storage silos and ensures that storage resources are used more efficiently. Furthermore, storage consolidation simplifies backup and recovery operations, as data can be stored in a centralized location and replicated to remote sites for redundancy.

Another important aspect of FCIP is its ability to integrate with other technologies, such as iSCSI and Fibre Channel over Ethernet (FCoE). While FCIP is specifically designed for Fiber Channel networks, it can be used in conjunction with other protocols to create hybrid storage environments that meet diverse business needs. For example, iSCSI is often used for storage in environments where cost is a concern, as it operates over standard Ethernet networks. By integrating FCIP with iSCSI, businesses can create a unified storage infrastructure that combines the performance benefits of Fiber Channel with the flexibility and cost-effectiveness of Ethernet-based protocols. Similarly, FCIP can be used alongside FCoE to create a converged network that carries both storage and data traffic over the same physical infrastructure.

Security is also a critical consideration when transmitting storage traffic over WANs. FCIP provides several mechanisms to ensure that data remains secure while in transit, including encryption and authentication. Encryption ensures that data is protected from unauthorized access while being transmitted over the WAN, preventing sensitive information from being intercepted. Authentication ensures that only authorized devices can connect to the FCIP network and exchange data, preventing unauthorized access to the storage infrastructure. These security measures are particularly important in industries such as healthcare, finance, and government, where data privacy and security are paramount.

FCIP also facilitates easier management of remote SANs, as it allows administrators to monitor and manage SAN traffic and devices over a unified management platform. By extending Fiber Channel networks over IP, administrators can use existing IP management tools and infrastructure to manage storage devices and troubleshoot issues, regardless of the geographical location of the devices. This simplifies network management and reduces the need for specialized, location-dependent management tools.

In summary, Fiber Channel over IP (FCIP) and its application in WAN connectivity provide organizations with the ability to extend their SANs over large distances while maintaining high performance, reliability, and security. By using FCIP, businesses can reduce the cost and complexity of deploying dedicated fiber optic connections, while still achieving the performance and data integrity benefits of Fiber Channel. FCIP enables critical use cases such as disaster recovery, data replication, and storage consolidation, all while providing the flexibility to integrate with other storage protocols. As organizations continue to expand and diversify their IT environments, FCIP will play an increasingly important role in enabling seamless, high-performance storage connectivity over wide-area networks.

# Fiber Channel Multiplexing and Routing

Fiber Channel is a high-speed, low-latency networking technology used primarily for storage area networks (SANs). In environments that require fast and reliable access to large amounts of data, Fiber Channel provides an effective and robust solution. One of the key features that contribute to the efficiency and scalability of Fiber Channel networks is its ability to support multiplexing and routing. Multiplexing and routing are essential techniques that allow Fiber Channel networks to manage data traffic efficiently across complex infrastructures, enabling data to travel over various paths, optimizing bandwidth, and ensuring redundancy. These techniques ensure that networks can handle high-performance requirements while maintaining the flexibility and fault tolerance needed for enterprise environments.

Multiplexing, in the context of Fiber Channel, refers to the technique of combining multiple data streams into one transmission medium or channel. This is essential for efficient utilization of available bandwidth. In Fiber Channel networks, multiplexing is achieved through techniques such as time-division multiplexing (TDM), which allows multiple data channels to share the same physical link while maintaining their individual data integrity. This approach ensures that the physical infrastructure is used effectively, as it reduces the need for additional cables and switches, which could otherwise increase both costs and complexity. By combining data from different sources into a single stream, multiplexing increases the overall capacity of the network, allowing more devices to communicate over fewer physical connections without compromising performance.

The benefits of multiplexing are particularly evident in large-scale SANs, where numerous servers and storage devices need to communicate simultaneously. Without multiplexing, each data stream would require a separate physical connection, which would not be efficient, particularly as the number of devices and data traffic grows. Multiplexing allows for better resource utilization, as it enables multiple data streams to be transmitted over a single Fiber Channel link. It also provides a level of flexibility, as network administrators can configure and adjust the network to meet evolving data demands without the need to overhaul the entire infrastructure. This makes multiplexing an important aspect of Fiber Channel design, particularly in environments where bandwidth demands are high.

Routing, on the other hand, is the process of directing data from its source to its destination across the network. In Fiber Channel networks, routing is essential for ensuring that data can be transmitted efficiently between devices across different segments of the SAN. Fiber Channel networks typically use switches to manage traffic and direct it to the appropriate destination. Routing in these networks involves determining the best path for data to take based on factors such as network topology, load balancing, and fault tolerance. Effective routing ensures that data can flow quickly and reliably between devices, even in large, complex SANs with multiple interconnected switches and storage devices.

In a typical Fiber Channel environment, the network is organized into a switched fabric, where multiple switches are interconnected, creating a mesh of paths that data can travel. Routing within this fabric is crucial for maintaining high availability and preventing data bottlenecks.

Fiber Channel routing protocols ensure that data packets are sent across the most efficient path, taking into account the current network conditions, including congestion and latency. In case of link or device failure, routing protocols also provide automatic failover, redirecting traffic to alternate paths to maintain network availability. This redundancy is particularly important in environments where downtime is not acceptable, such as in financial institutions, healthcare, or e-commerce platforms, where continuous data availability is a must.

Fiber Channel networks often use the Fabric Shortest Path First (FSPF) protocol for routing within a switched fabric. FSPF is a link-state protocol that calculates the shortest path for data to travel across the network based on the current topology and network conditions. By continuously updating its view of the network, FSPF ensures that data is always routed along the most optimal path, helping to minimize latency and maximize throughput. In the event of network changes, such as the failure of a link or the addition of a new device, FSPF quickly recalculates the routing paths to adapt to the new conditions, ensuring that data continues to flow efficiently across the network.

The combination of multiplexing and routing enables Fiber Channel networks to handle large volumes of data traffic while maintaining high performance and reliability. Multiplexing increases bandwidth efficiency by combining multiple data streams into a single transmission medium, while routing ensures that data travels across the most efficient paths, optimizing network resources and minimizing delays. The two techniques work together to create a scalable and flexible infrastructure that can grow with an organization's needs, handling increasing data demands without sacrificing performance.

One of the challenges in managing multiplexing and routing in Fiber Channel networks is ensuring that the network remains fault-tolerant and resilient to failure. In large-scale SANs, the risk of network failures increases, particularly as the number of devices and data flows grows. To address this, Fiber Channel networks incorporate redundancy and fault-tolerance mechanisms. For example, the use of multiple physical paths between devices allows data to be rerouted if one path fails, ensuring that the network remains operational. Additionally, the use of redundant switches and the implementation of multipathing techniques provide further layers of fault tolerance, ensuring that even in the event of hardware failures, the network can continue to function seamlessly.

Another key aspect of managing multiplexing and routing in Fiber Channel networks is ensuring security. As data travels across the network, it is essential to protect it from unauthorized access or tampering. Fiber Channel networks use various security measures, including zoning, encryption, and authentication, to secure data. Zoning is the practice of defining access policies that restrict which devices can communicate with one another within the SAN. Encryption ensures that data is protected during transmission, making it unreadable to unauthorized parties, while authentication verifies the identity of devices attempting to connect to the network. These security measures are especially important when routing data over large and potentially vulnerable networks, such as in cloud-based SANs or hybrid infrastructures.

The management of multiplexing and routing in Fiber Channel networks also involves constant monitoring and adjustment to ensure that the network continues to operate optimally. As data flows increase and new devices are added to the SAN, administrators must monitor network performance and make adjustments to the multiplexing and routing configurations to accommodate the changing demands. This might involve reallocating bandwidth, reconfiguring zoning policies, or adjusting routing protocols to ensure that data flows efficiently and that network resources are used effectively.

In conclusion, the integration of multiplexing and routing in Fiber Channel networks plays a crucial role in optimizing performance, ensuring scalability, and maintaining reliability in enterprise storage environments. Multiplexing allows for efficient use of available bandwidth, while routing ensures that data is transmitted along the most efficient and resilient paths. Together, these techniques enable Fiber Channel networks to handle large volumes of data traffic and provide the high-performance, fault-tolerant infrastructure required for modern business operations. By managing multiplexing and routing effectively, organizations can ensure that their Fiber Channel networks remain efficient, secure, and capable of supporting their growing data storage needs.

# Scaling Fiber Channel Networks for Large Environments

Scaling a Fiber Channel network for large environments is a critical consideration for enterprises that rely on high-performance, high-capacity storage solutions. As organizations grow, so do their data storage and access needs. Fiber Channel networks, with their ability to provide low-latency, high-throughput data transfer, are well-suited to meet the demands of large-scale, mission-critical applications. However, the challenge lies in expanding the network to accommodate increasing numbers of devices, users, and data without compromising performance, reliability, or security. Successfully scaling a Fiber Channel network requires careful planning, resource management, and an understanding of the specific requirements of the environment.

The first step in scaling a Fiber Channel network for large environments is understanding the infrastructure requirements. A large environment typically involves hundreds or even thousands of devices, including servers, storage devices, switches, and host bus adapters (HBAs). With such a complex array of components, network administrators must design the network with scalability in mind, ensuring that each part of the system can grow and adapt as demands increase. This begins with understanding the network's current bandwidth needs and projecting future growth. It is important to assess not only the volume of data that needs to be stored but also the speed at which data must be accessed, as well as the number of devices that will be connected to the network.

One of the primary considerations when scaling a Fiber Channel network is bandwidth. As the number of devices and the volume of data increase, so does the need for greater bandwidth. Fiber Channel operates at various speeds, typically ranging from 1Gbps to 128Gbps. Choosing the right speed for the network depends on the current and future demands. In large environments, it is often necessary to implement high-speed Fiber Channel technologies, such as 16Gbps or 32Gbps, to ensure that the network can handle the increased traffic without bottlenecks. Additionally, administrators must plan for future bandwidth requirements, as over-provisioning too much bandwidth can be inefficient and costly, while under-provisioning can lead to performance degradation and slow data access.

Once the bandwidth requirements are understood, administrators must also design the network topology to ensure it can scale efficiently. Fiber Channel networks typically use a switched fabric topology, where multiple switches interconnect devices, creating a mesh of redundant paths for data transmission. This topology is highly scalable and provides the redundancy necessary for fault tolerance. However, as the network grows, managing the switch fabric becomes more complex. In large environments, it is important to choose switches that can scale with the network, supporting the increased number of devices and maintaining low-latency communication. Additionally, the network must be designed to minimize congestion by ensuring that the traffic flows efficiently between devices and that the load is balanced across the network. This can be achieved by deploying multiple switches and implementing features such as load balancing and path optimization.

In large-scale Fiber Channel networks, redundancy is a crucial component of the design. As the network grows, the risk of hardware failures increases, and ensuring high availability becomes a priority. Redundancy is implemented through features such as multipathing, where multiple physical paths are provided between devices, ensuring that if one path fails, the data can continue to flow through another. Multipathing ensures that the network remains operational even in the event of hardware failures, minimizing downtime and ensuring continuous data access. Fiber Channel networks also support redundant switches and links, which further enhance fault tolerance. These redundant components ensure that if one switch or path fails, there are alternative paths for the data to travel, preventing disruptions in the network.

In large environments, the complexity of managing zoning increases significantly. Zoning in Fiber Channel networks is used to define access control policies, ensuring that only authorized devices can communicate with each other. As the number of devices increases, managing zoning becomes more challenging. The network must be segmented into smaller, manageable zones to prevent unnecessary traffic and ensure that devices only communicate with those they need to. This segmentation also helps improve security by isolating devices and restricting access to sensitive data. Automated zoning management tools can help streamline the process, allowing administrators to quickly configure and manage zones as the network expands. Effective zoning management ensures that the network remains secure, efficient, and easy to manage as it scales.

Another important consideration when scaling a Fiber Channel network is storage management. As the number of storage devices increases, so does the complexity of managing them. Storage resource management tools are essential for monitoring and allocating storage across the network. These tools provide administrators with the ability to view storage utilization, allocate resources dynamically, and monitor performance in real-time. In large environments, it is crucial to ensure that storage is used efficiently and that resources are not underutilized or overburdened. Storage virtualization techniques can also be employed to abstract the underlying physical storage and present a unified view of the storage resources. This makes it easier to manage large volumes of data and provides flexibility in allocating resources based on changing requirements.

Security is another critical aspect when scaling Fiber Channel networks. As the network expands, the risk of unauthorized access increases, and it becomes more difficult to maintain control over which devices and users have access to sensitive data. Fiber Channel networks provide several mechanisms for securing the network, including zoning, authentication, and encryption. Zoning ensures that devices are isolated into logical groups, reducing the risk of unauthorized access. Authentication mechanisms ensure that only trusted devices can join the network, preventing rogue devices from gaining access. Encryption can also be used to protect data as it travels across the network, ensuring that sensitive information remains secure even in the event of a breach. As the network scales, these security mechanisms must be carefully managed to ensure that the growing number of devices and users can be securely authenticated and authorized.

The management of a large Fiber Channel network requires robust tools and processes for monitoring, troubleshooting, and maintaining the network. As the number of devices and data traffic increases, the network must be continuously monitored to ensure optimal performance. Performance monitoring tools can track key metrics such as throughput, latency, and error rates, allowing administrators to detect issues before they impact the network. Additionally, automated network management systems can help streamline the configuration and monitoring of devices, reducing the complexity of managing large environments. These tools provide administrators with the visibility they need to ensure the network is operating efficiently and that issues are identified and resolved quickly.

Scaling a Fiber Channel network for large environments requires careful planning, resource allocation, and an understanding of the network's performance and security requirements. By addressing key factors such as bandwidth, network topology, redundancy, zoning, storage management, and security, administrators can ensure that the network can scale effectively to meet the demands of growing data and business requirements. A well-designed, scalable Fiber Channel network ensures that organizations can continue to meet the needs of modern applications while maintaining high performance, reliability, and security. As businesses continue to expand, scaling Fiber Channel networks will remain a critical consideration to ensure that storage infrastructures can support the growing demands of the enterprise.

# Redundancy and High Availability in Fiber Channel Networks

Fiber Channel networks are foundational to high-performance storage area networks (SANs) in enterprise environments. These networks support critical applications, providing fast, reliable access to data stored across multiple devices. Given the importance of these systems, ensuring the continued availability of data and the reliability of the network is paramount. Redundancy and high availability (HA) are integral concepts in the design and operation of Fiber Channel networks, ensuring that the network remains operational even in the event of hardware failures, link issues, or other disruptions. Properly implementing redundancy and HA strategies not only minimizes downtime but also enhances the performance and fault tolerance of the entire storage infrastructure.

Redundancy in Fiber Channel networks refers to the deliberate inclusion of duplicate components and pathways to eliminate single points of failure within the system. The goal of redundancy is to ensure that if one part of the network fails, data and services are not interrupted, and operations can continue as usual. In a typical Fiber Channel SAN, redundancy is implemented at multiple levels, including the physical links, switches, storage devices, and even the network topology itself. By having multiple paths and devices that can perform the same functions, Fiber Channel networks can achieve a high level of resilience.

One of the most fundamental methods for achieving redundancy in Fiber Channel networks is the use of multiple physical links. In a traditional, non-redundant network, a failure in a single cable or link could disrupt communication between devices, leading to data unavailability or downtime. Fiber Channel addresses this issue through the use of redundant paths. By employing multiple cables between devices and switches, data can be routed along the most efficient or alternate paths, ensuring that the network remains operational even if one link becomes unavailable. This is often referred to as multipathing, where several data paths are configured to increase fault tolerance and ensure continuous access to storage resources.

In addition to redundant physical links, Fiber Channel networks also benefit from redundant switches. Switches play a vital role in connecting devices within the network, routing data between storage devices and servers. A failure of a switch could potentially bring down a significant portion of the network, disrupting access to critical data. To mitigate this risk, network architects often design SANs with redundant switches. These switches can be configured in a way that, if one switch fails, traffic is automatically rerouted to another switch, allowing for seamless communication without any disruption to users or applications. Switch redundancy is a key part of building a highly available network, ensuring that no single switch failure can compromise the integrity or performance of the SAN.

Another layer of redundancy is provided at the storage device level. In large-scale Fiber Channel networks, storage devices, such as disk arrays or storage controllers, are often configured with redundant components, including multiple power supplies, disk drives, and controllers. This ensures that if one component of the storage system fails, another can take over without interrupting access to the data. Redundant controllers are typically employed in storage arrays to manage data access, so if one controller fails, the other can seamlessly assume control, ensuring that data remains accessible to the rest of the network.

To complement redundancy, high availability (HA) strategies are implemented to ensure the network is always available and responsive. HA in Fiber Channel networks typically involves the use of intelligent routing protocols and automated failover mechanisms. For example, the use of Fabric Shortest Path First (FSPF) protocol in Fiber Channel networks ensures that data is always sent via the shortest and least congested path within the fabric. If a failure occurs on one path, the FSPF protocol automatically recalculates the most optimal route for data traffic, ensuring that performance is maintained without interruption. The ability to rapidly switch to a backup route is essential for minimizing latency and maximizing throughput during times of failure.

High availability is also supported by multipathing, a key feature in ensuring fault tolerance and redundancy. Multipathing enables data to travel across multiple physical paths between the servers and storage devices. In the event that one of the paths fails, the data traffic can be automatically redirected to another path, preventing any disruption to service. In addition to providing fault tolerance, multipathing also helps balance network load by distributing traffic across available paths. This load balancing ensures that no single path becomes congested, improving overall network performance and increasing the efficiency of data transmission.

Redundancy and HA also require careful network design to prevent bottlenecks and optimize the flow of data across the network. The network topology, for instance, plays a crucial role in ensuring that the right amount of bandwidth is available to accommodate increased traffic and prevent delays. Fiber Channel networks commonly employ a switched fabric topology, where switches are interconnected to create a mesh of paths. This topology allows multiple devices to communicate with each other through various switches, and it inherently supports redundancy by providing multiple paths for data to travel. The design must ensure that enough bandwidth is allocated to handle traffic loads and that no part of the network becomes a potential point of failure.

Security is another critical consideration in maintaining the availability and integrity of a Fiber Channel network. Ensuring that redundant and highly available systems are not vulnerable to unauthorized access is essential for maintaining the trust and security of the network. Security protocols such as zoning and encryption are commonly employed in Fiber Channel networks to control access and protect sensitive data. Zoning allows administrators to create logical segments within the SAN, ensuring that devices in one zone cannot communicate with devices in another unless explicitly allowed. This adds a layer of security by preventing unauthorized access to critical data. Encryption is often used to protect data as it travels across the network, preventing interception and tampering during transmission.

Effective monitoring and management are also essential for ensuring the redundancy and availability of Fiber Channel networks. Continuous monitoring of the network can help identify potential failures before they escalate into major issues. By using management software, administrators can track the health of switches, links, storage devices, and other components, receiving alerts when issues arise. This proactive approach allows administrators to take corrective action, such as rerouting traffic, replacing failed components, or adjusting network configurations to restore service quickly.

The integration of disaster recovery strategies is a key part of ensuring high availability in Fiber Channel networks. By using techniques such as remote replication and data mirroring, organizations can ensure that copies of critical data are stored at remote sites. In the event of a network or data center failure, the data can be quickly restored from the replicated storage, minimizing downtime and ensuring business continuity. Fiber Channel networks are particularly well-suited for disaster recovery due to their high-speed capabilities, which enable real-time or near-real-time replication of large volumes of data.

Redundancy and high availability are vital components in the design and operation of Fiber Channel networks. These techniques ensure that data remains accessible, secure, and uninterrupted, even in the event of hardware failures or network disruptions. By implementing redundant paths, switches, storage devices, and failover mechanisms, organizations can build resilient networks that continue to function efficiently and reliably, even under adverse conditions. The combination of redundancy and high availability enables businesses to meet the growing demands of modern applications while ensuring the performance and security of their critical storage infrastructure.

# SAN Failover Mechanisms and Automatic Recovery

In modern Storage Area Networks (SANs), ensuring the continuous availability of data is a fundamental requirement for businesses that rely on high-performance and mission-critical applications. As data grows in volume and importance, even small amounts of downtime can result in significant operational and financial losses. In this context, failover mechanisms and automatic recovery processes are crucial for maintaining the stability and reliability of SAN environments. These mechanisms help ensure that SANs remain operational even in the face of hardware failures, network issues, or other disruptions. Understanding how failover and recovery work in SANs is essential for maintaining a resilient and high-availability storage infrastructure.

At its core, failover refers to the ability of a SAN to automatically switch to a backup system or path in the event of a failure. The goal is to minimize downtime and ensure that data access is not interrupted when a component or connection in the network fails. Failover mechanisms are often built into the architecture of the SAN, ensuring that if one part of the system goes down, the load can be shifted seamlessly to another operational component without user intervention. This automatic switching is crucial for organizations that require continuous access to data, such as in the financial sector, healthcare, or e-commerce, where even brief interruptions can lead to data loss or significant service disruption.

One of the most common forms of failover in SANs is the use of redundant paths. In a typical SAN setup, multiple physical paths connect the servers, switches, and storage devices. This redundancy ensures that if one path fails due to a hardware issue, another path can be used without disrupting service. Redundant paths are a key component of Fiber Channel SANs, where the use of multipathing software allows the system to automatically detect and reroute data through an alternative path. For example, if a cable fails or a switch goes down, the SAN can continue to operate normally by using one of the other available paths. This dynamic path selection improves the reliability of the network and reduces the risk of data loss or access delays.

In addition to path redundancy, failover mechanisms are also built into the storage devices themselves. Modern storage systems often have dual controllers, each capable of managing the data access independently. If one controller fails, the other takes over the responsibility of managing the storage, ensuring that the data remains available without interruption. This type of storage controller redundancy is often used in high-availability environments where downtime is unacceptable. Dual controllers in storage arrays can work in an active-active or active-passive configuration. In an active-active setup, both controllers are working simultaneously, sharing the load. If one controller fails, the other continues to provide access to the data without any disruption. In an active-passive configuration, only one controller is active at a time, with the passive controller standing by to take over in case of failure. Both configurations ensure that the storage system remains operational even in the event of hardware failure.

Automatic recovery mechanisms are essential for ensuring that the SAN not only survives a failure but also returns to full operation without requiring manual intervention. Recovery in a SAN context involves restoring the system to its normal state after a failure has been detected and resolved. This process can include re-establishing network paths, recovering data, or resuming interrupted processes. Automatic recovery is often triggered by the failover mechanism when it detects a failure and takes corrective action to restore services. For example, if a path fails and traffic is rerouted through another available path, the failover process ensures that no data is lost and that the data stream continues without interruption. Once the failed component is restored, the system automatically switches back to the optimal path, ensuring that traffic flows through the most efficient route.

The success of automatic recovery mechanisms in SANs depends on a combination of monitoring, detection, and response systems. Monitoring tools play a crucial role in identifying potential issues before they lead to failures. These tools constantly check the health of the components within the SAN, such as switches, storage devices, and links. When a problem is detected, such as a performance degradation or an error in a component, administrators are alerted immediately, allowing them to take corrective actions proactively. If the issue escalates into a failure, the failover mechanism takes over, ensuring that operations continue seamlessly. Monitoring tools also help track the status of recovery after failover, ensuring that the system is fully operational and that no data has been lost in the process.

In addition to hardware-based redundancy and failover mechanisms, many modern SAN environments also incorporate software-based recovery solutions. These solutions are particularly important for managing large-scale, distributed SANs where multiple locations or data centers are involved. Software solutions, such as remote replication and snapshots, allow data to be copied to a secondary site in real-time or on a scheduled basis. If a failure occurs at the primary site, the secondary site can take over, ensuring that the data remains available and consistent. Remote replication, for example, continuously updates the data at a remote site, making it immediately available if the primary SAN experiences an outage. Snapshots create point-in-time copies of data, enabling rapid recovery of critical data without affecting ongoing operations.

One of the significant challenges in implementing failover and automatic recovery in SANs is ensuring that these mechanisms are transparent to users and applications. When a failure occurs, it is essential that end-users or applications do not experience any disruption in their ability to access data. For this reason, SAN administrators must design and configure the failover mechanisms to operate seamlessly, ensuring that data is available without noticeable delay. This requires careful planning of the network topology, redundancy, and automatic recovery processes to ensure that all components of the SAN work together harmoniously. Testing these systems regularly is also crucial, as it allows administrators to ensure that failover and recovery processes function as expected under various failure scenarios.

As organizations increasingly move to virtualized environments, the complexity of failover and recovery in SANs grows. Virtual machines (VMs) rely on shared storage in the SAN to function properly. When a failure occurs in a SAN, it can affect multiple VMs running on different servers. Virtualized environments require additional failover mechanisms to ensure that VM data is not lost and that VMs can be quickly recovered after a failure. Solutions like VMware Site Recovery Manager and Microsoft Hyper-V Replica can be integrated with SANs to automate the recovery of virtualized environments, minimizing the downtime and ensuring business continuity.

In conclusion, failover mechanisms and automatic recovery are fundamental to ensuring the resilience and availability of Fiber Channel SANs in modern IT environments. By incorporating redundancy at multiple levels, including paths, storage devices, and switches, SANs can withstand failures without significant disruption. Automatic recovery ensures that the system can return to normal operation swiftly, minimizing downtime and preventing data loss. With continuous monitoring, advanced software solutions, and well-planned failover strategies, SANs can provide the high availability and fault tolerance required to support the critical applications and data needs of modern enterprises.

# Integrating Fiber Channel Networks with Cloud Storage

The integration of Fiber Channel networks with cloud storage represents a critical evolution in how organizations manage their data infrastructure. As businesses face growing data demands, the ability to seamlessly combine high-performance on-premise storage systems, such as those provided by Fiber Channel networks, with scalable cloud storage solutions has become increasingly important. Fiber Channel, known for its low-latency and high-throughput capabilities, is a proven technology for enterprise environments. On the other hand, cloud storage offers flexibility, scalability, and cost-efficiency, allowing organizations to store vast amounts of data with minimal on-site infrastructure. Integrating these two distinct technologies allows businesses to leverage the strengths of both, creating a hybrid environment that supports the evolving needs of modern data management.

Fiber Channel networks provide high-speed, dedicated connections between storage devices and servers, which is essential for applications that require rapid access to large amounts of data. The technology excels in environments where performance and reliability are paramount, such as in data centers, financial institutions, and healthcare systems. However, while Fiber Channel networks offer outstanding performance, they are limited by their on-premise infrastructure, which can be costly to scale. As organizations' data needs continue to expand, the demand for flexible and cost-effective storage solutions has led many to explore cloud storage as a complement to their existing Fiber Channel setups.

Cloud storage offers several advantages over traditional on-premise storage systems, such as unlimited scalability, reduced capital expenditure, and the ability to store data in geographically distributed locations. These benefits make cloud storage particularly attractive for businesses looking to manage large volumes of data without the need for significant physical infrastructure investments. However, the challenge lies in integrating cloud storage with existing on-premise Fiber Channel environments to ensure that the two systems can work together seamlessly. By combining the performance benefits of Fiber Channel with the scalability and flexibility of cloud storage, organizations can create a hybrid storage infrastructure that meets both their current and future data needs.

One of the primary methods of integrating Fiber Channel networks with cloud storage is through the use of Fiber Channel over Ethernet (FCoE) technology. FCoE allows for the transport of Fiber Channel frames over Ethernet networks, bridging the gap between traditional Fiber Channel networks and cloud-based storage systems. FCoE provides a unified fabric that can carry both storage and network traffic, making it easier to integrate with cloud platforms that rely on Ethernet-based connections. This integration simplifies the overall network infrastructure and reduces the complexity of managing separate storage and network systems. By leveraging FCoE, organizations can extend their Fiber Channel networks to cloud environments, ensuring that data flows seamlessly between on-premise and cloud storage resources.

In addition to FCoE, another key technology for integrating Fiber Channel with cloud storage is the use of cloud gateways. Cloud gateways act as intermediaries between on-premise Fiber Channel networks and cloud storage platforms. These devices provide a secure and efficient means of transferring data between the two environments, enabling businesses to move data to the cloud while maintaining the performance benefits of Fiber Channel. Cloud gateways typically support multiple storage protocols, including Fiber Channel, iSCSI, and NFS, making it easier to connect diverse storage systems to the cloud. By using cloud gateways, organizations can maintain their existing Fiber Channel infrastructure while expanding their storage capacity to the cloud, effectively creating a hybrid storage solution.

The integration of Fiber Channel with cloud storage also requires a comprehensive data management strategy to ensure that data is appropriately allocated and stored across both on-premise and cloud environments. For example, organizations may choose to keep high-performance data, such as databases or active files, on local Fiber Channel storage, while offloading less critical or archival data to the cloud. This tiered storage approach allows businesses to optimize performance and cost-efficiency by ensuring that the most frequently accessed data remains on-premise, while less-used data is stored in the cloud. Many cloud storage providers offer tiered storage options that automatically move data between different classes of storage based on access frequency, helping businesses manage costs while ensuring that their data is always accessible.

Data security and compliance are also critical considerations when integrating Fiber Channel with cloud storage. Many organizations must adhere to strict regulatory requirements regarding data privacy and security, particularly in industries such as healthcare, finance, and government. Ensuring that sensitive data is securely transferred and stored across on-premise and cloud environments is essential for maintaining compliance. Encryption is one of the key tools used to protect data during transit and at rest. When integrating Fiber Channel with cloud storage, it is important to implement end-to-end encryption to protect sensitive information as it moves between the two environments. Additionally, many cloud providers offer encryption and compliance certifications, ensuring that businesses can meet regulatory requirements when storing data in the cloud.

Another important aspect of integration is ensuring that the performance of the overall system meets the demands of business-critical applications. While cloud storage offers significant scalability, the performance of data transfer between on-premise Fiber Channel systems and the cloud can be impacted by factors such as bandwidth, latency, and network congestion. To mitigate these challenges, organizations can implement strategies such as data caching and compression to improve the speed and efficiency of data transfers between the cloud and local storage systems. By caching frequently accessed data on-premise, organizations can reduce the need to repeatedly access the cloud, improving performance and reducing network load.

One of the key advantages of integrating Fiber Channel with cloud storage is the ability to implement a robust disaster recovery strategy. Cloud storage inherently offers geographic redundancy, meaning that data stored in the cloud is often replicated across multiple data centers in different locations. This replication ensures that data is protected in the event of a hardware failure or natural disaster. By extending their Fiber Channel networks to the cloud, businesses can leverage this geographic redundancy to enhance their disaster recovery capabilities. In the event of a data center failure, data can be quickly recovered from the cloud, minimizing downtime and ensuring business continuity. Furthermore, cloud-based disaster recovery solutions can be more cost-effective than maintaining dedicated off-site storage or backup systems.

The integration of Fiber Channel networks with cloud storage also enables greater flexibility and agility in managing data. As businesses scale their operations and their data storage needs grow, they can seamlessly expand their storage capacity in the cloud without the need for significant capital investment in on-premise infrastructure. This scalability allows organizations to keep pace with increasing data demands, supporting both short-term and long-term business growth. Additionally, cloud storage provides the flexibility to quickly adapt to changing business requirements, such as fluctuating data volumes or new regulatory compliance standards.

In summary, integrating Fiber Channel networks with cloud storage enables organizations to combine the performance benefits of on-premise Fiber Channel systems with the scalability and cost-effectiveness of cloud storage. By using technologies such as FCoE, cloud gateways, and tiered storage, businesses can create a hybrid storage environment that supports their data management needs while reducing costs and complexity. Security, compliance, and performance are critical considerations when integrating these two technologies, but with the right strategies and tools in place, organizations can create a flexible, high-performance storage infrastructure that meets both their current and future needs. This integration opens up new possibilities for businesses to manage, protect, and scale their data while leveraging the power of the cloud.

# Compatibility Considerations for Fiber Channel Networks

Fiber Channel networks are integral to providing high-performance, reliable, and scalable storage solutions for enterprise environments. However, as with any complex technology, integrating Fiber Channel networks into an organization's existing IT infrastructure requires careful consideration of compatibility. Fiber Channel networks must be able to seamlessly interoperate with a variety of devices, protocols, and storage systems across the network. Compatibility issues, if not addressed early on, can lead to performance bottlenecks, connectivity problems, or even system failures. Ensuring that all components of the Fiber Channel network are compatible with one another, as well as with other systems such as servers, switches, storage arrays, and network infrastructure, is essential for maintaining a stable and efficient storage environment.

One of the primary considerations when deploying Fiber Channel networks is ensuring compatibility between the various components involved. Fiber Channel is a protocol used to transfer data between devices in a Storage Area Network (SAN), and it typically involves several layers, including the physical layer, the link layer, and the protocol layer. At each layer, compatibility must be considered to ensure smooth communication between devices. For example, when selecting switches and host bus adapters (HBAs), it is important to verify that the devices support the same version of the Fiber Channel protocol. Fiber Channel technology evolves over time, with new versions offering faster speeds, more reliable connections, and enhanced features. However, newer devices and technologies may not always be backward-compatible with older systems, which can lead to interoperability issues. Ensuring compatibility across different generations of hardware is a critical step in maintaining the integrity and efficiency of the network.

Fiber Channel also operates at various speeds, such as 1Gbps, 4Gbps, 8Gbps, 16Gbps, and 32Gbps. Each version provides different levels of performance, with higher speeds allowing for greater data transfer rates and improved overall network performance. When upgrading or expanding a Fiber Channel network, compatibility with existing equipment at different speeds must be considered. While newer Fiber Channel devices are often backward-compatible with older systems, mixing different speeds on the same network may result in performance degradation or inefficiencies. For instance, if a network includes both 8Gbps and 16Gbps devices, the overall performance may be limited to the speed of the slower components unless proper adjustments, such as link negotiation, are made. Therefore, organizations must carefully plan the upgrade process to ensure that speed mismatches do not hinder network performance.

Another important aspect of compatibility in Fiber Channel networks is the physical connectivity between devices. Fiber Channel networks rely heavily on fiber optic cabling, and the type of fiber cable used must be compatible with the devices in the network. Fiber optic cables come in various forms, including single-mode and multi-mode fiber. Single-mode fiber is typically used for long-distance connections, while multi-mode fiber is more commonly used for shorter distances. When designing a Fiber Channel network, it is essential to ensure that the correct type of fiber optic cable is chosen to meet the distance and performance requirements of the network. Additionally, the connectors used to interface with fiber optic cables must be compatible with the devices in the network. Common connector types include LC, SC, and MTP/MPO, and using the wrong connector type can prevent the devices from communicating properly. Compatibility issues with cabling and connectors can lead to unreliable connections, poor network performance, and increased troubleshooting efforts.

In addition to physical components, the network topology plays a significant role in ensuring compatibility within a Fiber Channel network. Fiber Channel networks are often implemented using a switched fabric topology, where multiple switches are interconnected, creating a mesh of paths for data to travel between devices. This topology allows for high scalability and redundancy, but it also introduces the need for careful consideration of compatibility between switches and other network devices. Different switch manufacturers may implement the Fiber Channel protocol in slightly different ways, which could lead to issues if devices from different vendors are mixed within the same fabric. Ensuring that switches from different vendors are compatible requires careful review of technical specifications, firmware versions, and vendor certifications. Additionally, it may be necessary to perform testing to verify that the switches are interoperating properly before fully deploying the network.

Compatibility with storage devices is another critical factor to consider when deploying Fiber Channel networks. Fiber Channel networks are commonly used to connect servers to storage arrays, and ensuring that the storage devices are compatible with the Fiber Channel protocol is essential for seamless data access. Many modern storage systems are designed to work with multiple protocols, including Fiber Channel, iSCSI, and FCoE (Fiber Channel over Ethernet), which allows them to support a variety of network configurations. However, it is important to verify that the storage devices support the specific version and speed of Fiber Channel used in the network. Additionally, storage arrays often have their own management tools and protocols that need to be compatible with the network's configuration. Misalignments in management protocols or incompatibilities between the storage system and the network could result in slower data access times, difficulty in managing storage resources, or even system failure. To mitigate these risks, careful validation and compatibility testing should be conducted before integrating new storage devices into the network.

As organizations increasingly adopt virtualization technologies, compatibility with virtualized environments becomes a significant consideration in Fiber Channel network deployments. Virtualized servers rely on shared storage systems, often connected through Fiber Channel networks, to access the data required for running virtual machines. Compatibility issues can arise when integrating Fiber Channel with virtualization platforms like VMware or Microsoft Hyper-V. For example, certain versions of Fiber Channel HBAs may not be fully supported by the virtualization platform or the associated management tools. Additionally, issues can arise when trying to map virtual machine storage to the physical storage in a SAN. Ensuring that the appropriate virtual storage drivers, such as VMware's Virtual Machine File System (VMFS) or similar software, are in place is critical for ensuring that virtualized environments run efficiently and securely on a Fiber Channel network.

Fiber Channel networks also need to be compatible with various network management and monitoring tools. These tools are essential for ensuring the performance, security, and reliability of the network. Network management tools for Fiber Channel often provide features such as fault detection, performance monitoring, and resource allocation, but they must be compatible with the specific devices and configurations in the network. This includes ensuring that the management software supports the correct firmware versions of switches, HBAs, and storage arrays. Compatibility with monitoring protocols, such as SNMP, is also important for maintaining network visibility and troubleshooting issues.

Lastly, the integration of Fiber Channel networks with other technologies, such as cloud storage or software-defined networking (SDN), requires special attention to compatibility. As businesses increasingly move to hybrid cloud environments, ensuring that their on-premise Fiber Channel networks can interface with cloud storage solutions is critical for managing data across distributed infrastructures. Similarly, the integration of SDN with Fiber Channel networks requires ensuring that the network can support dynamic traffic routing, load balancing, and automation without disrupting the performance or reliability of the SAN.

In any large or complex deployment, compatibility considerations for Fiber Channel networks require thorough planning and testing. Misconfigurations, mismatched versions, or incompatible hardware and software components can undermine the performance and stability of the entire network. By addressing compatibility concerns early in the planning process and conducting rigorous testing, organizations can ensure that their Fiber Channel networks will support their storage needs both now and in the future. Compatibility is not just about avoiding errors, but about creating a seamless, high-performing, and reliable storage infrastructure capable of supporting the demands of modern enterprise environments.

# Fiber Channel SANs in Virtualized Environments

The integration of Fiber Channel Storage Area Networks (SANs) in virtualized environments is a powerful combination that delivers high-performance, reliable, and scalable storage solutions for modern data centers. As businesses adopt virtualization technologies to improve resource utilization, reduce costs, and enhance flexibility, the demand for high-speed storage solutions that can handle large volumes of data while maintaining low latency has grown significantly. Fiber Channel SANs, with their dedicated, high-throughput communication capabilities, provide the perfect foundation for supporting virtualized environments, enabling enterprises to scale their storage infrastructure efficiently while meeting the performance demands of virtual machines (VMs) and other virtualized workloads.

A virtualized environment typically involves the consolidation of multiple physical servers and their resources into a smaller number of powerful, multi-tenant virtual machines. Each virtual machine requires access to shared storage resources, and ensuring that these VMs have fast and reliable access to data is critical for maintaining the performance and stability of the overall system. Fiber Channel SANs are ideal for virtualized environments because they offer the necessary bandwidth, reliability, and low-latency data transfer that VMs require to operate efficiently. By providing centralized storage that can be shared by multiple virtual machines, Fiber Channel SANs help simplify storage management and improve resource utilization, both of which are essential for the success of virtualized environments.

One of the primary benefits of using Fiber Channel SANs in virtualized environments is the ability to provide consistent and predictable performance. Virtualized workloads, especially those running mission-critical applications, require fast and uninterrupted access to data. Fiber Channel's high-speed connectivity, typically ranging from 8Gbps to 32Gbps, ensures that storage access does not become a bottleneck in the virtualized environment. With Fiber Channel SANs, organizations can allocate storage resources based on the needs of each VM, ensuring that high-performance applications receive the bandwidth and low-latency access they require, while lower-priority workloads are allocated fewer resources. This flexibility and efficiency in resource allocation are key to maximizing the performance of virtualized environments.

Furthermore, Fiber Channel SANs allow for the centralized management of storage resources. In a virtualized environment, storage is often shared by many VMs, and the ability to manage storage centrally provides several advantages. Administrators can allocate storage resources dynamically, responding to changes in workload demand without the need for physical intervention. Fiber Channel SANs can be easily integrated with virtualization platforms, such as VMware or Microsoft Hyper-V, to provide automated provisioning of storage for virtual machines. This integration simplifies storage management, reduces administrative overhead, and ensures that VMs are provided with the necessary storage resources on demand.

Another advantage of using Fiber Channel SANs in virtualized environments is the high availability and fault tolerance they offer. In enterprise environments, ensuring that data is always available is paramount, and downtime can have significant financial and operational consequences. Fiber Channel SANs are designed with redundancy and failover mechanisms built into the fabric, ensuring that the network remains operational even if one or more components fail. Features like multipathing, redundant links, and dual-active storage controllers allow Fiber Channel SANs to provide a high level of fault tolerance. In a virtualized environment, these capabilities ensure that virtual machines remain accessible, even in the event of hardware failures. If one path to the storage array becomes unavailable, multipathing allows traffic to be rerouted through another path, minimizing the risk of downtime. This resilience is essential in environments where business continuity is critical.

In addition to redundancy and failover, data protection is another key concern in virtualized environments. Fiber Channel SANs provide robust data protection features, such as snapshots, replication, and backup solutions, which are essential for safeguarding virtual machine data. Snapshots allow administrators to create point-in-time copies of storage volumes, which can be used for quick recovery in case of data corruption or other issues. Replication enables data to be mirrored between geographically dispersed data centers, providing disaster recovery capabilities in case of site failures. These data protection features help organizations ensure that their virtualized environments are resilient to data loss and can quickly recover from failures, minimizing the impact of disruptions.

As virtualized environments grow in complexity, managing and scaling storage resources can become increasingly challenging. Fiber Channel SANs provide a scalable solution that can grow with the needs of the business. The flexibility of Fiber Channel SANs allows organizations to add storage capacity as needed without disrupting operations. Whether through the addition of new storage devices or the expansion of the SAN fabric, Fiber Channel networks are designed to scale efficiently. This scalability is particularly important in virtualized environments, where the number of virtual machines and storage demands can increase rapidly. By using Fiber Channel SANs, businesses can ensure that their storage infrastructure can scale with their virtualized workloads, supporting growing data requirements and helping to avoid potential performance bottlenecks.

Security is another important consideration when integrating Fiber Channel SANs with virtualized environments. Virtual machines often store sensitive data, and protecting this data from unauthorized access is critical for maintaining compliance with regulations and ensuring the integrity of the organization's IT systems. Fiber Channel networks provide several security mechanisms, such as zoning, authentication, and encryption, to ensure that only authorized devices can access storage resources. Zoning allows administrators to isolate devices into different groups, restricting access to specific portions of the SAN. Encryption ensures that data is protected during transmission, making it unreadable to unauthorized parties. These security features help safeguard data in virtualized environments, reducing the risk of data breaches and ensuring compliance with industry standards.

The integration of Fiber Channel SANs with virtualized environments also enhances storage efficiency through technologies such as thin provisioning and storage virtualization. Thin provisioning allows administrators to allocate storage resources dynamically, providing VMs with the storage they need while minimizing unused capacity. This ensures that storage is used more efficiently, reducing waste and optimizing resource utilization. Storage virtualization enables the abstraction of physical storage devices, presenting a unified view of the storage pool to virtual machines. This simplifies storage management by allowing administrators to manage storage as a logical unit rather than individual physical devices. By integrating these technologies with Fiber Channel SANs, organizations can create more efficient, cost-effective storage environments that meet the needs of their virtualized workloads.

As businesses continue to adopt virtualized environments, the demand for flexible, high-performance storage solutions will only increase. Fiber Channel SANs provide the scalability, reliability, and performance required to meet the evolving demands of these environments. By offering high-speed data access, fault tolerance, centralized storage management, and robust data protection, Fiber Channel SANs are well-suited to support the dynamic and growing needs of virtualized infrastructures. The ability to seamlessly integrate with virtualization platforms and support emerging technologies such as storage virtualization and thin provisioning further strengthens the case for Fiber Channel as the storage solution of choice in virtualized environments. By combining the power of Fiber Channel with virtualization, organizations can build a storage infrastructure that is both efficient and highly available, enabling them to respond quickly to changing business needs.

# Automation in SAN Management

The management of Storage Area Networks (SANs) has become increasingly complex due to the growing volume of data, the increasing number of devices, and the need for high availability and performance. As organizations continue to scale their storage infrastructures, manual management processes are no longer sufficient to handle the demands of modern data centers. Automation in SAN management offers an efficient and scalable solution to these challenges by allowing for the dynamic configuration, monitoring, and optimization of storage resources. By automating various aspects of SAN management, organizations can reduce operational overhead, improve consistency, and ensure that storage resources are utilized effectively, while also maintaining high levels of performance and availability.

One of the primary reasons automation has become critical in SAN management is the rapid expansion of data and the increasing number of devices that need to be managed. As businesses rely more heavily on data-driven applications, the amount of data generated and stored grows exponentially. In traditional, manually managed environments, administrators would need to manually configure each device, allocate storage resources, and monitor the performance of each component. This process is time-consuming and prone to human error, making it increasingly difficult to maintain a consistent and efficient SAN. Automation streamlines these tasks by allowing systems to automatically handle repetitive and time-consuming processes, freeing up administrators to focus on more strategic activities.

Automation can be applied to various aspects of SAN management, including provisioning, configuration, performance monitoring, and troubleshooting. One of the most significant benefits of automation is the ability to streamline the provisioning of storage resources. In traditional environments, provisioning storage would require administrators to manually allocate storage volumes to servers and configure each device. This process can be slow and inefficient, especially in large-scale SAN environments with many devices. With automation, storage provisioning can be simplified by using predefined policies and templates that automatically allocate the appropriate amount of storage to servers based on their needs. These policies can take into account factors such as the type of application, the required performance levels, and the available storage capacity, ensuring that resources are allocated efficiently and consistently.

Another area where automation plays a key role is in the configuration and management of the SAN fabric. In large SANs, which may consist of hundreds or thousands of switches and storage devices, manually configuring each device can be an overwhelming task. Automation tools can be used to simplify this process by automatically configuring switches, zoning, and other elements of the SAN fabric. For example, zoning, which defines which devices can communicate with each other within the SAN, is a critical component of SAN security and performance. In a manual environment, administrators would need to configure each zone individually, which can be time-consuming and prone to mistakes. With automation, zoning can be automatically defined based on device types, access policies, or performance requirements, ensuring that the correct devices are grouped together without manual intervention.

Performance monitoring and optimization are also critical components of SAN management. As data flows through the SAN, administrators need to ensure that performance remains consistent and that potential bottlenecks are quickly identified and addressed. Manually monitoring the performance of each device and path in the network is time-consuming and inefficient. Automation tools allow administrators to set performance thresholds and receive real-time alerts when these thresholds are breached. Automated performance monitoring can track key metrics such as throughput, latency, and error rates across the entire SAN, providing administrators with a holistic view of the network's health. If a bottleneck is detected or a device is underperforming, automation systems can trigger predefined corrective actions, such as rerouting traffic or allocating additional resources, to mitigate performance degradation.

In addition to performance monitoring, automation can also be used to simplify troubleshooting and fault resolution. When issues arise in a SAN, such as a failed device or degraded performance, administrators need to quickly identify the root cause of the problem and take corrective action. In manual environments, this often requires sifting through logs and diagnostic data, which can be time-consuming and complex. Automation tools can help streamline this process by providing real-time diagnostics and automatically identifying potential issues. For example, if a switch fails or a storage device becomes unavailable, automation systems can automatically detect the failure and trigger predefined actions, such as switching to a redundant path or notifying administrators of the issue. This enables faster response times and minimizes downtime by quickly addressing problems before they escalate.

Another important area where automation plays a critical role is in the management of storage capacity. As organizations scale their storage environments, it becomes increasingly difficult to ensure that resources are being used efficiently and that capacity is not being over-provisioned or under-utilized. Manual tracking of storage usage can lead to inefficiencies and wasted resources. Automation tools can provide real-time visibility into storage utilization and automatically adjust resource allocation based on usage patterns. For example, if a particular storage array is nearing full capacity, automation systems can move data to other arrays or provision additional storage to meet demand. This ensures that storage resources are used efficiently and that businesses can avoid costly over-provisioning while ensuring that they have the capacity they need to support growing workloads.

Security is also a key consideration in SAN management, and automation can play a role in enhancing security by enforcing policies and responding to potential threats. Automation tools can be used to enforce zoning policies, ensuring that only authorized devices are allowed to communicate within the SAN. Additionally, automation can help with auditing and compliance by tracking user access and configuration changes across the network. If unauthorized access attempts are detected, automated systems can trigger security alerts or take corrective actions, such as blocking access to sensitive data or requiring additional authentication. By automating security enforcement, organizations can reduce the risk of human error and ensure that security policies are consistently applied across the SAN.

In addition to the technical benefits, automation in SAN management also leads to operational efficiency. As the volume of data and the number of devices in the network continue to grow, the need for skilled administrators also increases. However, by automating routine tasks, organizations can reduce the administrative workload and enable their staff to focus on higher-level tasks such as strategic planning and capacity forecasting. This can lead to significant cost savings by reducing the need for manual intervention and allowing staff to work more efficiently.

Automation tools are also increasingly integrated with cloud-based management platforms, which offer the ability to manage SAN resources in hybrid and multi-cloud environments. As organizations adopt cloud storage and services, it is essential to have the ability to integrate these resources with on-premise SANs seamlessly. Automation makes this integration possible by providing a consistent interface for managing storage across both on-premise and cloud-based systems. This allows businesses to create flexible and scalable storage environments that can adapt to changing demands, such as shifting workloads to the cloud during peak times or expanding on-premise storage as needed.

In the rapidly evolving world of enterprise storage, automation has become an indispensable tool for SAN management. By automating provisioning, configuration, performance monitoring, troubleshooting, and security, organizations can reduce complexity, improve consistency, and ensure the efficient use of resources. As the size and scale of storage environments continue to grow, automation will play a critical role in enabling organizations to maintain high-performance SANs that can meet the increasing demands of modern applications and business operations. With the right automation tools in place, businesses can not only reduce operational costs but also enhance the overall performance and reliability of their storage infrastructure.

# Future Trends in Fiber Channel and SAN Technology

As data continues to grow at an exponential rate, the need for efficient, high-performance storage systems has never been more crucial. Fiber Channel (FC) and Storage Area Networks (SANs) have long been the backbone of enterprise data centers, providing the speed, reliability, and scalability required to meet the demands of modern applications. However, as the technology landscape evolves, Fiber Channel and SAN technologies are undergoing significant transformations to keep up with new business needs, cloud integration, virtualization, and the ever-growing volume of data. The future of these technologies is shaped by several emerging trends that focus on improving performance, simplifying management, enhancing security, and integrating with newer technologies such as artificial intelligence (AI) and machine learning (ML).

One of the most significant trends in Fiber Channel and SAN technology is the continued push for higher speeds. As organizations require faster data transfer rates to handle increasingly complex workloads, Fiber Channel technology is advancing to provide higher throughput and reduced latency. While the current standard for Fiber Channel is 32Gbps, there is already a push towards the adoption of 64Gbps and even 128Gbps. These advancements in speed will be crucial for supporting applications such as big data analytics, real-time data processing, and high-performance computing, which require extremely fast and efficient data transfer. With higher speeds, Fiber Channel can meet the demands of data-heavy applications, enabling faster data access and reducing bottlenecks within SAN environments.

In addition to higher speeds, another critical trend is the move towards more efficient and automated management of SANs. As data centers grow in complexity and scale, managing the numerous devices, connections, and storage resources manually becomes increasingly difficult. The future of SAN technology lies in automation, with new management tools being developed to streamline configuration, monitoring, and troubleshooting processes. Automation will not only simplify the management of large-scale SANs but also improve performance by reducing human error and ensuring that resources are allocated more efficiently. Technologies such as software-defined storage (SDS) and intelligent automation are already beginning to play a larger role in the management of SANs, enabling dynamic adjustments based on workload demands, real-time data, and predictive analytics.

Virtualization is another significant trend shaping the future of Fiber Channel and SAN technologies. As organizations continue to virtualize their data centers, the storage requirements of virtual machines (VMs) are becoming more complex. Virtualization enables businesses to maximize resource utilization, but it also creates new challenges for storage, as VMs require shared access to storage resources. Fiber Channel SANs are uniquely suited to meet these challenges, providing centralized storage that can be accessed by multiple VMs. The future of Fiber Channel in virtualized environments will involve deeper integration with hypervisors and virtualization platforms such as VMware and Microsoft Hyper-V. Newer versions of Fiber Channel, such as Fiber Channel over Ethernet (FCoE), allow SANs to work seamlessly in environments that leverage both storage and network traffic over the same Ethernet infrastructure. This hybrid approach is expected to grow in the coming years, as businesses seek more integrated solutions for both storage and networking.

Cloud integration is also a crucial area of development for Fiber Channel and SAN technologies. As organizations increasingly adopt hybrid cloud architectures, the need for seamless integration between on-premise SANs and cloud storage solutions is paramount. Fiber Channel networks are typically confined to on-premise environments, but as cloud adoption continues to rise, the future of SANs will involve hybrid models that combine the performance and reliability of traditional Fiber Channel with the scalability and flexibility of cloud storage. Cloud gateways and software-defined storage platforms are emerging as key enablers of this integration, allowing data to be seamlessly transferred between on-premise SANs and public or private cloud environments. This hybrid storage model will provide businesses with the ability to scale their storage resources dynamically, while still maintaining the high performance and low latency required for mission-critical applications.

One of the most exciting future trends in Fiber Channel and SAN technology is the incorporation of artificial intelligence (AI) and machine learning (ML) to optimize storage performance. AI and ML algorithms can analyze large volumes of data and identify patterns, anomalies, and potential inefficiencies within the SAN. This can lead to smarter data placement, real-time performance adjustments, predictive maintenance, and the automation of routine management tasks. For instance, AI can predict when a storage device is likely to fail, allowing administrators to take proactive measures to prevent downtime. Additionally, machine learning can help optimize data traffic within the SAN, ensuring that data is routed along the most efficient paths and minimizing bottlenecks. These technologies will be increasingly integrated into SAN management software, providing administrators with more intelligent tools to optimize storage performance and ensure high availability.

Security is another critical area of focus for the future of Fiber Channel and SAN technologies. As data becomes more valuable and cyber threats become more sophisticated, securing storage networks is paramount. Fiber Channel networks, traditionally seen as more secure due to their isolated nature, will continue to evolve to address new security challenges. Future Fiber Channel technologies will likely incorporate stronger encryption methods, both for data at rest and in transit, to ensure that sensitive information remains protected even if the network is compromised. Additionally, security policies will become more integrated into the SAN infrastructure itself, with automated compliance and access control features becoming more prevalent. As the number of connected devices in SAN environments grows, implementing zero-trust security models and more granular access controls will become essential to safeguarding against unauthorized access.

The shift towards more sustainable and energy-efficient technologies is also expected to impact the future of Fiber Channel and SANs. As organizations strive to reduce their carbon footprint and energy consumption, there will be an increased demand for storage solutions that are both high-performance and energy-efficient. Advances in hardware, such as low-power switches and storage devices, will help to meet these sustainability goals. In addition, energy-efficient network protocols and software optimizations will contribute to reducing the environmental impact of SANs. With the growing importance of environmental sustainability, the integration of energy-efficient practices into Fiber Channel SANs will be a significant trend in the coming years.

Finally, the evolution of Fiber Channel and SAN technology will be shaped by the ongoing convergence of storage, networking, and computing resources. In the future, Fiber Channel will likely be integrated more closely with other network technologies such as

Ethernet, enabling more flexible and cost-effective storage solutions. The rise of software-defined networking (SDN) and storage virtualization will further blur the lines between traditional storage networks and more agile, software-driven architectures. This convergence will enable businesses to create more flexible and scalable storage infrastructures that can adapt to the changing needs of modern applications, such as big data analytics, artificial intelligence, and edge computing.

The future of Fiber Channel and SAN technologies is characterized by a continued push for higher performance, greater automation, deeper cloud integration, and enhanced security. As data demands continue to rise, the evolution of these technologies will be crucial in ensuring that organizations can manage and store their data efficiently, securely, and cost-effectively. The integration of AI, machine learning, and more energy-efficient practices will further optimize SAN operations, creating smarter, more sustainable storage environments capable of supporting the next generation of applications and services. As these trends unfold, Fiber Channel SANs will continue to play a pivotal role in the ever-evolving landscape of enterprise IT infrastructure.

# The Role of Fiber Channel in Modern Data Centers

Fiber Channel technology has long been a cornerstone of high-performance storage in enterprise environments, and its role in modern data centers remains indispensable. In today's data-driven world, where organizations handle massive volumes of data and require constant access to information, the need for fast, reliable, and scalable storage solutions is more pressing than ever. Fiber Channel provides these essential capabilities by offering a dedicated, high-speed, and low-latency communication pathway for data storage and retrieval. As data centers become increasingly complex and critical to business operations, the role of Fiber Channel in supporting large-scale, mission-critical applications continues to evolve.

In modern data centers, storage needs have become significantly more demanding. With the proliferation of cloud computing, virtualization, big data analytics, and high-performance applications, the performance of storage networks is a top priority. Fiber Channel networks are designed to meet these performance requirements by delivering high-speed data transfer rates, reliability, and low latency. Unlike traditional IP-based networking technologies, Fiber Channel operates on its own dedicated fabric, ensuring that storage traffic is separated from general network traffic. This isolation improves the overall performance of the network by preventing congestion and reducing the impact of non-storage-related activities. The high throughput and low latency of Fiber Channel are crucial for environments that rely on real-time data access, such as financial institutions, healthcare providers, and online services that require immediate access to large datasets.

One of the key strengths of Fiber Channel is its ability to provide predictable and consistent performance, even as the volume of data increases. Modern data centers are often home to large-scale virtualization environments, where hundreds or even thousands of virtual machines (VMs) are hosted on a shared infrastructure. These virtualized environments place a significant burden on storage systems, as multiple VMs simultaneously access data from a central storage repository. Fiber Channel SANs are ideal for these scenarios because they provide the dedicated bandwidth and low-latency access required by virtual machines. As more applications are virtualized, Fiber Channel remains a reliable solution to support these resource-intensive workloads, ensuring that VMs have the fast and efficient access to storage they need to function effectively.

In addition to high performance, Fiber Channel also offers superior reliability, which is critical in a data center environment. Modern data centers are built with redundancy and high availability in mind, ensuring that services remain operational even if hardware or network components fail. Fiber Channel supports redundancy at multiple levels, including network paths, switches, and storage devices. The use of redundant paths between storage devices and servers ensures that if one path fails, data can still be accessed through another path, reducing the risk of downtime. Fiber Channel networks also support features such as multipathing and failover, which automatically redirect traffic to available paths in case of a failure. This built-in resilience ensures that modern data centers remain highly available, even in the face of hardware failures or network issues.

As data center environments become increasingly virtualized, the ability to manage and scale storage resources efficiently is critical. Fiber Channel SANs provide centralized storage that can be dynamically allocated to different virtual machines as needed. The integration of Fiber Channel with virtualization platforms such as VMware and Microsoft Hyper-V allows storage to be managed more effectively, ensuring that virtualized workloads receive the appropriate storage resources based on their performance and capacity requirements. This centralized approach to storage management not only simplifies provisioning and scaling but also enhances the efficiency of resource utilization. Organizations can add storage capacity as needed, without the need for significant reconfiguration or disruption to services, ensuring that the data center infrastructure can scale to meet growing business demands.

In modern data centers, security is also a primary concern, as organizations must protect sensitive data from unauthorized access, breaches, and cyberattacks. Fiber Channel networks provide a higher level of security compared to traditional IP-based storage systems. Because Fiber Channel operates on a dedicated network fabric, it is inherently more isolated from other network traffic, reducing the risk of external threats. Additionally, Fiber Channel supports advanced security features such as zoning, which allows administrators to define access control policies and restrict which devices can communicate within the SAN. Zoning ensures that only authorized devices can access sensitive data, adding an additional layer of security to the storage infrastructure. Encryption is also becoming an increasingly important feature in Fiber Channel, ensuring that data is protected while in transit across the network.

The integration of Fiber Channel with cloud environments is another growing trend in modern data centers. As organizations increasingly adopt hybrid cloud architectures, the ability to connect on-premise storage to cloud-based storage solutions has become essential. Fiber Channel is well-suited to support hybrid environments, as it offers the high performance and reliability required for mission-critical workloads. By extending Fiber Channel SANs to the cloud, organizations can ensure that their storage infrastructure is scalable and flexible, allowing them to move data seamlessly between on-premise systems and the cloud. Cloud gateways and Fiber Channel over Ethernet (FCoE) are emerging technologies that enable the integration of on-premise Fiber Channel networks with cloud storage platforms, making it easier for businesses to manage their data across both on-site and cloud-based systems.

In addition to cloud integration, the rise of data-intensive technologies such as artificial intelligence (AI) and machine learning (ML) has further solidified the role of Fiber Channel in modern data centers. These technologies require access to massive amounts of data, often in real-time, and the performance demands placed on storage systems are substantial. Fiber Channel SANs, with their high-speed data transfer capabilities, are ideal for supporting AI and ML applications, which rely on fast access to large datasets for training models and running inference tasks. The ability to quickly process and retrieve data is crucial in these environments, and Fiber Channel provides the low-latency and high-throughput required to keep up with the demands of AI and ML workloads.

In the coming years, Fiber Channel will continue to play a central role in the evolving landscape of data centers. As new technologies such as 5G, edge computing, and the Internet of Things (IoT) drive the need for faster and more reliable data access, Fiber Channel's ability to provide high-speed, low-latency connectivity will be essential for supporting the next generation of applications. Fiber Channel's dedicated nature and ability to handle high-bandwidth traffic make it uniquely suited to support the demands of future data centers, where data will continue to grow exponentially, and the need for performance and reliability will only increase.

The future of Fiber Channel in modern data centers is intertwined with the growth of virtualization, cloud computing, AI, and other emerging technologies. Fiber Channel will continue to provide the high performance, reliability, and scalability that enterprises require as they manage increasingly complex IT infrastructures. The ability to integrate with cloud environments, support virtualized workloads, and handle next-generation data applications will ensure that Fiber

Channel remains a crucial component in the storage architecture of modern data centers for years to come.

# Data Migration Strategies in Fiber Channel SANs

Data migration within Fiber Channel Storage Area Networks (SANs) plays a critical role in modern data management strategies. As organizations grow, their storage needs evolve, requiring them to transition data across different storage platforms, environments, or configurations. Whether the goal is to upgrade storage hardware, consolidate data, or extend storage capabilities into the cloud, effective data migration is essential for ensuring minimal downtime, optimal performance, and the continued availability of critical data. Fiber Channel SANs, with their high-performance, low-latency capabilities, provide a robust infrastructure for supporting data migration, but careful planning and execution are required to ensure that the migration process is seamless, secure, and efficient.

The first step in any data migration process is to assess the current environment and establish clear goals for the migration. Organizations must determine why they are migrating data, what data will be moved, and how the migration will impact the overall SAN infrastructure. Factors such as the volume of data to be migrated, the types of storage systems involved, and the desired downtime window must be considered before developing a migration strategy. A thorough assessment will allow organizations to identify potential challenges, such as network bandwidth limitations, storage capacity constraints, or compatibility issues between different generations of storage systems. The more comprehensive the initial assessment, the smoother the migration process will be.

When migrating data within a Fiber Channel SAN, one of the most critical considerations is the impact on performance. Data migration can put a significant load on the network, especially in large-scale SAN environments where multiple terabytes or even petabytes of data need to be moved. Migrating data during peak usage times can lead to congestion, slow access to data, and potential performance degradation across the SAN. To mitigate these risks, many organizations choose to schedule migrations during off-peak hours or weekends when network activity is lower. Additionally, data can be migrated in stages to avoid overloading the system. By breaking the migration process into smaller, more manageable chunks, organizations can minimize the impact on daily operations while still ensuring that the migration is completed within the required timeframe.

The type of data migration method chosen is also crucial in determining how efficiently the process will unfold. There are two primary approaches to data migration: online and offline migration. Online migration allows data to be moved while applications continue to run, which is essential for businesses that require continuous data availability. In an online migration, data is copied from the source storage system to the target storage system while maintaining read and write access to the source system. Once the data transfer is complete, any changes made to the source data during the migration are synchronized with the target storage system. This method is ideal for environments that cannot afford significant downtime, such as those supporting mission-critical applications.

Offline migration, on the other hand, involves taking the storage system offline while the data is moved to the target system. While this method ensures that the migration process is clean and free from conflicts, it requires scheduled downtime, which may not be acceptable for all organizations. This approach is more suited to less time-sensitive data or when the migration window allows for extended downtime. The choice between online and offline migration will depend on the specific needs of the organization, including the required level of data availability, the volume of data being migrated, and the complexity of the SAN infrastructure.

Another important consideration during data migration is the integrity and security of the data being transferred. Ensuring that data remains intact and secure during the migration process is paramount, especially when migrating sensitive information or business-critical data. Data integrity checks, such as hash-based verifications, should be performed regularly throughout the migration process to ensure that no corruption occurs during the transfer. Additionally, encryption should be used to protect data during transit, particularly when moving data between different physical locations or over long distances. Many Fiber Channel SAN environments already include built-in encryption capabilities, but additional security measures, such as secure tunnels or virtual private networks (VPNs), may be necessary when migrating data over external networks.

In large SAN environments, where multiple devices, switches, and storage arrays are involved, compatibility between different generations of hardware and software is a critical concern. For example, organizations may need to migrate data from an older Fiber Channel SAN to a newer one with different performance characteristics, hardware, or storage protocols. Compatibility testing should be conducted before initiating the migration to ensure that all devices in the SAN can communicate effectively with the target storage systems. Fiber Channel SANs typically support backward compatibility between different generations of hardware, but compatibility issues can arise, especially if the systems use different versions of the Fiber Channel protocol or storage devices with varying capacities and configurations.

To manage the complexity of data migration in Fiber Channel SANs, many organizations leverage specialized migration tools and software. These tools automate and streamline many of the tasks involved in the migration process, including data transfer, integrity verification, and synchronization. Migration tools can help reduce manual errors, speed up the process, and provide real-time visibility into the progress of the migration. Some advanced migration tools also offer built-in failover mechanisms, ensuring that if an issue occurs during the migration, the process can be paused and resumed without significant disruption. These tools are especially valuable in large, complex SAN environments, where multiple systems must be integrated and managed during the migration process.

Data migration in Fiber Channel SANs also requires careful planning regarding the target storage architecture. As organizations increasingly embrace cloud computing, hybrid storage models that combine on-premise SANs with cloud storage are becoming more common. In such scenarios, the migration strategy must take into account the differences between local and cloud storage systems, including performance, security, and access protocols. While cloud storage provides flexibility and scalability, it may not always offer the same level of performance or low latency as Fiber Channel SANs. Therefore, businesses must determine which data should remain on-premise and which data can be offloaded to the cloud. The migration strategy should include clear policies for data tiering, ensuring that performance-sensitive data remains on-premise, while less frequently accessed or archival data can be moved to the cloud.

Another factor to consider during migration is the preservation of metadata and file attributes. In many environments, data is not just stored as raw files but with associated metadata that describes its structure, relationships, and access permissions. Ensuring that this metadata is preserved during migration is vital for maintaining data integrity and application performance. Special care should be taken when migrating databases or other applications that rely on metadata to function properly. Failing to preserve metadata during migration can lead to data corruption, access issues, or application failures, which can significantly impact the business.

In conclusion, data migration in Fiber Channel SANs is a complex, multifaceted process that requires careful planning, robust tools, and strong attention to detail. Organizations must consider factors such as migration type, hardware compatibility, data integrity, and security to ensure a smooth and efficient transition. With the right strategies and technologies in place, organizations can successfully migrate their data, optimize their storage resources, and position themselves for future growth and scalability. Fiber Channel SANs continue to provide a reliable and high-performance foundation for data migration, supporting the increasing demands of modern enterprises and enabling them to manage and store their data effectively.

# Fiber Channel for Big Data and High-Performance Computing

In the world of data-driven enterprises, high-performance computing (HPC) and big data analytics have become integral to unlocking insights, improving decision-making, and maintaining competitive advantage. To support these resource-intensive workloads, data centers require robust, scalable, and high-performance storage solutions. Fiber Channel, with its proven reliability, low-latency, and high-throughput capabilities, plays a pivotal role in meeting the performance demands of both big data environments and HPC applications. These two fields, driven by vast amounts of data and complex computations, demand storage solutions that can provide high-speed access, efficient data management, and seamless scalability. Fiber Channel SANs (Storage Area Networks) offer a solution that aligns perfectly with these requirements, providing a stable foundation for high-performance applications and large-scale data analysis.

Big data environments generate vast quantities of structured and unstructured data, with organizations seeking to analyze this data to gain insights into customer behavior, business trends, scientific research, and more. However, managing and processing this data presents significant challenges, particularly around speed and scalability. The need for fast data access is critical, as data is continuously ingested from various sources, analyzed, and transformed to extract value. Traditional storage technologies may struggle to meet the throughput and latency requirements of these environments, especially as data volume and processing complexity grow. Fiber Channel SANs address these challenges by providing a dedicated, high-performance network for data storage that operates independently of general-purpose network traffic. This isolation ensures that big data workloads receive the required performance, without the risk of congestion or delays caused by unrelated network traffic.

In a big data context, the performance of the storage infrastructure is paramount. Fiber Channel's high-speed data transfer rates, ranging from 8Gbps to 128Gbps, are ideal for environments where large datasets need to be accessed, processed, and analyzed in real-time. The low-latency nature of Fiber Channel ensures that data is retrieved quickly, supporting time-sensitive big data operations such as data streaming, real-time analytics, and complex queries. Whether it is processing large datasets for machine learning models or analyzing data from IoT devices in real-time, Fiber Channel provides the necessary bandwidth and speed to maintain high performance across multiple applications. With big data solutions requiring massive parallel data access, Fiber Channel networks excel by supporting multiple data paths that enable simultaneous access to data across distributed storage systems. This ensures that no single point of contention hinders data access speed, crucial for big data applications where downtime or delays are unacceptable.

The demand for high-throughput and low-latency access is similarly critical in high-performance computing environments. HPC workloads typically involve simulations, complex calculations, and large-scale data processing, often in fields such as scientific research, engineering, and financial modeling. These applications require storage systems that can keep up with the rapid data processing needs, as well as high bandwidth to move data between storage and computing nodes efficiently. In HPC environments, every microsecond counts, and the network infrastructure that links storage to compute nodes must be capable of handling the enormous data volumes generated by the simulations. Fiber Channel SANs provide the necessary speed and reliability to ensure that large datasets can be read and written to storage devices without significant delays. The high throughput of Fiber Channel ensures that data can be transferred between compute nodes and storage devices at the required rate, allowing for real-time processing and faster results.

One of the key advantages of Fiber Channel SANs in both big data and HPC environments is their ability to scale as data and workload demands grow. As big data and HPC applications continue to evolve, the amount of data that needs to be processed and stored increases. Fiber Channel's scalability allows data centers to expand their storage infrastructure as needed, supporting the growth of data volumes without compromising performance. Fiber Channel networks are designed to be highly flexible, allowing for the addition of new storage devices, switches, and computing nodes without disrupting the existing network. This scalability is critical for big data and HPC environments, where the volume of data being generated and the computational power required can change rapidly. As such, Fiber Channel SANs can seamlessly accommodate future demands, supporting both the increased storage capacity and the higher-speed connections required by modern workloads.

Security is also a significant consideration in both big data and HPC environments, where data integrity and confidentiality are paramount. Fiber Channel networks offer enhanced security compared to traditional IP-based storage networks. The isolated, private nature of Fiber Channel SANs provides an added layer of security, reducing the potential exposure to network vulnerabilities that could otherwise compromise sensitive data. In addition, Fiber Channel supports features such as zoning, which enables network administrators to define access control policies and isolate critical storage devices from other parts of the network. These security mechanisms are particularly important in big data environments, where the storage of sensitive data—such as customer information, financial records, or proprietary research—requires stringent protection measures. Fiber Channel's ability to implement granular security policies at the network level ensures that only authorized users and devices can access the storage resources, protecting data from unauthorized access and cyber threats.

Another key factor that enhances the role of Fiber Channel in big data and HPC environments is its ability to provide a consistent and predictable network performance. With these applications being highly sensitive to latency and throughput, Fiber Channel's dedicated, high-performance infrastructure ensures that the network is optimized to handle the volume and velocity of data. Unlike traditional Ethernet networks, where network traffic can become congested with other types of communication, Fiber Channel networks are designed solely for storage traffic. This specialization ensures that high-performance workloads are not impacted by unrelated traffic, and data can be processed and accessed without delay. Moreover, Fiber Channel SANs offer advanced management tools that enable administrators to monitor and optimize storage performance, further ensuring that big data and HPC applications continue to run efficiently and without interruptions.

Cloning is another important data service available in SANs, providing an exact copy of a storage volume or virtual machine (VM). While snapshots are typically used for backup or disaster recovery, cloning is often used for data migration, testing, and load balancing. A clone is a full, writable copy of the original data, which can be used independently from the original dataset. This makes clones valuable in scenarios where data needs to be replicated for other purposes, such as creating testing environments or moving data between different storage systems. Unlike snapshots, which are usually read-only and represent a specific point in time, clones are live copies that can be modified, allowing businesses to perform testing or other operations without impacting the original data.

One common use case for cloning is in software testing. Developers may need to test applications against a copy of the production environment to ensure that new code or updates do not introduce bugs or issues. By using a clone of the production data, developers can run tests without putting the live environment at risk. Similarly, clones can be used in data migration projects, where data needs to be moved from one storage system to another without downtime or service interruptions. Cloning ensures that a consistent, accurate copy of the data is available for migration, while the original system continues to operate as usual.

Replication is another key data service in SAN environments, providing a way to copy data from one storage system to another, typically for purposes of disaster recovery, business continuity, and load balancing. Unlike snapshots and clones, which capture data at specific points in time, replication creates a continuous or near-continuous copy of the data. Replication can occur synchronously or asynchronously, depending on the requirements of the business.

In synchronous replication, data is written to both the primary and secondary storage systems simultaneously, ensuring that both copies are always in sync. This is typically used in mission-critical environments where real-time data protection is required. If the primary storage system experiences a failure, the secondary system can immediately take over without data loss, ensuring that operations continue without disruption. Synchronous replication, however, may introduce some latency because the data must be written to both systems before the write is considered complete.

Asynchronous replication, on the other hand, writes data to the primary system first and then replicates the changes to the secondary system at a later time. This type of replication is more efficient for large datasets and geographically distributed environments, as it does not require the data to be written to both systems at the same time. Asynchronous replication introduces a slight delay between the time data is written to the primary system and the time it is replicated, but it allows for greater flexibility and efficiency in terms of bandwidth usage.

Replication in SANs is often used for disaster recovery, enabling businesses to have an up-to-date copy of their data at a remote site. In the event of a failure at the primary site, the secondary system can take over, ensuring that data is still available and that business operations can continue. Many organizations use replication as part of their business continuity plans, ensuring that data is replicated across different geographic locations to protect against natural disasters, power outages, or other site-specific failures. Replication can also be used for load balancing, as the secondary storage system can be used to offload read requests or to distribute data access across multiple sites, improving performance and reducing the load on the primary storage system.

All three data services—snapshots, cloning, and replication—offer unique benefits that can help businesses manage and protect their data more effectively. While snapshots provide an efficient way to back up data at specific points in time, clones offer flexibility for testing, development, and migration. Replication, on the other hand, ensures data availability and resilience by continuously copying data to secondary systems. These services can be used independently or together, depending on the specific requirements of the organization.

The integration of these data services within a SAN environment also enables organizations to achieve more sophisticated data management and protection strategies. By automating the creation of snapshots, clones, and replication, businesses can streamline their data protection processes, ensuring that data is backed up, available, and recoverable in the event of a failure. Additionally, these services can be integrated with other IT management and orchestration tools, providing a centralized platform for managing data services across the enterprise.

As the volume of data continues to grow, the need for efficient, scalable, and reliable data services will only increase. Modern SAN technologies, with their advanced snapshot, cloning, and replication capabilities, are well-positioned to meet these challenges, ensuring that businesses can protect and manage their data effectively. Whether for backup, disaster recovery, or data migration, these services are critical to ensuring that organizations can continue to operate smoothly in an increasingly data-centric world.

# Troubleshooting Common Fiber Channel Issues

Fiber Channel technology has long been a cornerstone of high-performance, low-latency storage area networks (SANs), providing enterprises with a robust infrastructure for managing vast amounts of data. However, like any complex technology, Fiber Channel systems are prone to various issues that can affect performance, availability, and data integrity. Troubleshooting these issues is a crucial skill for network administrators and IT professionals, as resolving problems quickly and efficiently ensures the continued operation of mission-critical applications and minimizes downtime. Understanding the most common Fiber Channel issues and knowing how to diagnose and address them is key to maintaining a stable and performant storage environment.

One of the most common issues in Fiber Channel networks is connectivity problems. These problems often arise when devices within the SAN are unable to communicate with one another, typically due to physical layer issues. Cable faults are one of the primary culprits in connectivity problems. Fiber optic cables can be susceptible to damage, misalignment, or improper installation, all of which can cause communication failures. Network administrators should always ensure that the cables are properly connected, free from physical damage, and are the correct type for the specific Fiber Channel configuration. If a cable appears intact but still causes connectivity issues, administrators may need to use tools like an optical time-domain reflectometer (OTDR) to check for signal loss or cable faults. Additionally, verifying the integrity of connectors is critical, as improperly seated or dirty connectors can result in signal degradation or a complete loss of connectivity.

Another factor contributing to connectivity problems is the Fiber Channel switch configuration. If a device is unable to connect to the SAN, administrators should first check the switch settings. Switches are often configured to handle specific zoning rules, which control which devices are allowed to communicate with one another. Misconfigured zoning can lead to devices being isolated from one another, preventing them from establishing a connection. This can be particularly problematic in environments where multiple zones or virtual SANs (VSANs) are used. Zoning issues can typically be resolved by reviewing the zone configurations and ensuring that all devices are properly assigned to the correct zones. Administrators can use SAN management tools to view and modify zoning settings, ensuring that no devices are incorrectly isolated.

Link speed mismatches between devices are also a common source of connectivity issues in Fiber Channel networks. Fiber Channel devices, such as host bus adapters (HBAs) and switches, operate at various speeds, such as 8Gbps, 16Gbps, or 32Gbps. If two devices are configured to operate at different speeds, they may be unable to communicate effectively. In these cases, it is essential to ensure that both devices are set to compatible speeds, or that auto-negotiation is enabled to allow them to automatically agree on a speed that both devices can support. Mismatched speeds can lead to slow performance or even a complete failure to establish a connection, so it is important to verify the speed settings when troubleshooting connectivity issues.

Fiber Channel SANs are also vulnerable to performance degradation, often caused by congestion, overloaded links, or excessive latency. Performance issues can manifest as slow data transfers, timeouts, or high latency, all of which can significantly impact the performance of applications relying on the SAN. One of the primary causes of performance degradation is congestion in the network. As SANs grow in size and scale, network traffic can become increasingly complex, and data may struggle to flow efficiently between devices. Congestion can occur at various points in the SAN, including at the switch level, in the fiber optic cables, or even within the storage devices themselves. To diagnose congestion, administrators should use performance monitoring tools to track key metrics such as throughput, latency, and error rates. These tools can help pinpoint areas of the network where congestion is occurring, allowing for targeted remediation, such as adding additional bandwidth, optimizing routing, or upgrading devices.

Buffer credits are another factor that can impact Fiber Channel network performance. In Fiber Channel networks, buffer credits control the flow of data between devices to prevent data loss and ensure reliable communication. If buffer credits are not properly configured or are exhausted, it can lead to data loss or significant performance degradation. Buffer credit issues can often be traced back to switch configurations or misaligned settings between devices. Administrators should verify that buffer credits are properly allocated to avoid performance bottlenecks, especially in high-traffic environments.

Intermittent connectivity and performance issues may also be related to Fiber Channel loop problems. In loop configurations, multiple devices are connected in a circular manner, with each device acting as both a sender and receiver of data. These loops are vulnerable to a variety of issues, such as failed devices or improper termination, which can lead to data packet loss or network congestion. One common issue is the failure to properly terminate a loop, which can cause signals to bounce back and create interference in the network. To troubleshoot loop problems, administrators should check for devices that may be malfunctioning or improperly connected, as well as ensure that all loops are correctly terminated.

Another common problem in Fiber Channel networks is related to firmware and driver compatibility. Just like any other complex system, the devices in a Fiber Channel SAN rely on a combination of hardware and software that must work together seamlessly. Firmware bugs or outdated drivers can cause a variety of issues, including connectivity problems, performance degradation, and device failures. Network administrators should regularly check for firmware updates and ensure that all devices in the SAN are running the latest versions of their respective firmware and drivers. This can help prevent compatibility issues and ensure that the network operates at peak performance.

Security-related issues, such as unauthorized access or data breaches, are also concerns in Fiber Channel SANs. Although Fiber Channel networks are more secure than traditional IP-based storage networks due to their isolated nature, they are still vulnerable to potential threats. Misconfigured zoning, for example, can allow unauthorized devices to access sensitive data, while weak authentication methods can enable rogue devices to connect to the network. To prevent security breaches, administrators should enforce strict zoning policies, use strong authentication methods, and regularly audit the SAN for security vulnerabilities. Encryption of data in transit is another important security measure to protect sensitive information from being intercepted during communication across the SAN.

Finally, it is important to address hardware failures when troubleshooting Fiber Channel networks. Hardware issues, such as failing switches, HBAs, or storage devices, can result in system downtime, data unavailability, and reduced performance. When diagnosing hardware failures, administrators should use diagnostic tools to identify faulty components and replace them promptly. It is also essential to maintain redundant hardware, such as additional switches or backup devices, to minimize the impact of hardware failures on overall system availability.

Troubleshooting Fiber Channel issues requires a systematic and methodical approach. By identifying common issues such as connectivity problems, performance degradation, and hardware failures, and using the appropriate diagnostic tools, administrators can quickly resolve issues and maintain the reliability of the SAN. Understanding the underlying causes of these problems and implementing best practices for SAN management, including regular firmware updates, proper configuration, and proactive monitoring, can help prevent many common issues and ensure a stable, high-performance storage environment.

# SAN Backup Strategies: Implementing Fiber Channel Storage Solutions

In today's data-driven world, ensuring the integrity, availability, and protection of data is paramount. Storage Area Networks (SANs) have become the backbone of modern data centers, providing high-performance, scalable, and reliable storage solutions. However, as organizations increasingly rely on SANs to store critical business data, implementing an effective backup strategy becomes more essential than ever. Fiber Channel SANs, with their dedicated, high-speed network infrastructure, offer the ideal environment for backing up large volumes of data quickly and efficiently. However, designing and implementing backup strategies within Fiber Channel storage environments requires careful planning, a clear understanding of business needs, and an in-depth knowledge of SAN technology.

One of the key advantages of using Fiber Channel SANs for backup purposes is the high-speed data transfer rates they provide. Fiber Channel is known for its ability to deliver fast, low-latency connectivity, making it suitable for environments where large volumes of data need to be transferred quickly and reliably. The speed and performance of Fiber Channel SANs help ensure that backups can be performed with minimal disruption to day-to-day operations. In a typical SAN environment, backup data can be quickly replicated from primary storage to secondary storage arrays, providing up-to-date copies of business-critical data.

When implementing backup strategies for Fiber Channel SANs, one of the most important factors to consider is redundancy. Redundant copies of data ensure that if one storage system fails, another can quickly take over. In the context of backup, redundancy typically involves creating multiple copies of data, stored either on-premise or off-site, to ensure that a backup is always available in the event of data corruption, accidental deletion, or a complete storage failure. Fiber Channel SANs offer high availability and fault tolerance, ensuring that data can be reliably transferred and stored without risk of data loss. By incorporating redundancy into backup strategies, businesses can achieve a higher level of protection for their data.

For effective backup management, it is crucial to determine the right backup frequency and schedule. In many organizations, data changes constantly, and the frequency at which backups are taken will depend on the criticality of the data being stored. For example, transactional data in financial institutions or real-time customer data in e-commerce environments may require frequent or even continuous backups. Less critical data, such as archival or historical information, may not need to be backed up as often. One approach to addressing this is incremental backups, which only capture the changes made since the last backup, reducing the amount of data that needs to be transferred and stored. This approach ensures that backups are both efficient and comprehensive, without overwhelming the network or storage resources. Full backups can also be scheduled periodically to ensure that a complete, up-to-date copy of the data is always available.

Snapshot-based backups are another essential strategy for backing up data in Fiber Channel SANs. Snapshots are point-in-time copies of data volumes that are taken without interrupting ongoing operations. The ability to create a snapshot of a storage volume in a SAN environment allows businesses to back up their data almost instantaneously. Unlike traditional backup methods, which can require a lengthy process to copy and store data, snapshots can be taken in a fraction of the time, enabling near-continuous backup with minimal performance impact. Snapshot-based backups are particularly useful in environments where large datasets need to be protected without incurring significant downtime or performance degradation.

However, while snapshots provide a quick and efficient way to back up data, they also come with certain limitations. Snapshots typically capture only the state of the data at a specific point in time, and while they can be useful for short-term protection, they are not a complete replacement for full backups. Snapshots often rely on copy-on-write technology, meaning that any changes made to the data after the snapshot is taken are stored separately. This can result in storage overhead and increased complexity over time as the number of snapshots grows. To address this, organizations should implement strategies to manage snapshot retention, periodically deleting older snapshots and consolidating backup data as needed to maintain an efficient and organized storage structure.

Replication is another important backup strategy in Fiber Channel SANs, especially for disaster recovery purposes. Replication involves creating an exact copy of data from one storage system to another, typically at a remote location, ensuring that data is available in case of a site failure. Fiber Channel SANs support both synchronous and asynchronous replication, each with its advantages and trade-offs. Synchronous replication ensures that data is written to both the primary and secondary storage systems simultaneously, providing a real-time copy of the data. This type of replication is ideal for mission-critical applications where zero data loss is unacceptable. However, synchronous replication can introduce latency, particularly over long distances, due to the need to synchronize data across systems. Asynchronous replication, on the other hand, allows data to be written to the primary system first and then replicated to the secondary system at a later time. This method is more efficient for large datasets and long-distance replication, but it introduces a slight delay between the original data write and its replication. Both methods have their place in a comprehensive backup strategy, depending on the organization's data availability and performance requirements.

In addition to traditional backup methods, businesses are increasingly turning to cloud storage for off-site backups. The scalability and flexibility of cloud storage make it an attractive option for businesses that need to store large volumes of backup data without investing in additional physical infrastructure. Cloud storage can be integrated with Fiber Channel SANs to provide seamless, secure, and scalable backup solutions. By leveraging cloud-based backup solutions, organizations can take advantage of virtually unlimited storage capacity, ensure that data is stored off-site for disaster recovery, and benefit from the cloud provider's own redundancy and security measures. However, there are considerations around data transfer speed, security, and cost that businesses must take into account when incorporating cloud storage into their backup strategy.

Security is another critical aspect of SAN backup strategies. Backing up sensitive data requires robust encryption to ensure that data remains protected both during transit and while at rest. Fiber Channel SANs offer several security features, such as zoning and authentication, that help protect data from unauthorized access. In addition, integrating encryption technologies into the backup process ensures that data is protected against potential breaches or theft. Encryption can be applied to backup data both in the SAN environment and during transmission to remote or cloud-based storage locations, ensuring that sensitive information remains secure at all times.

Efficient management of backup data is also essential for maintaining the performance and scalability of the storage environment. With the vast amounts of data that are backed up in a modern SAN environment, managing backup sets, retention policies, and storage capacity can become complex. Using backup management software to automate the backup process and establish policies for data retention, verification, and archiving helps streamline the process and ensure that backup operations run smoothly. Furthermore, regular testing of backup processes is critical to ensure that data can be restored quickly and accurately in the event of a disaster.

As the volume and importance of data continue to grow, implementing a comprehensive backup strategy using Fiber Channel SANs is essential for organizations looking to ensure business continuity, data protection, and disaster recovery. By leveraging the high-performance capabilities of Fiber Channel, businesses can design efficient, reliable, and secure backup solutions that meet their growing data protection needs. Whether through snapshots, replication, or cloud storage integration, Fiber Channel SANs provide a solid foundation for organizations to safeguard their most valuable asset: their data.

# Compliance and Regulatory Requirements in SAN Environments

As organizations continue to store and manage vast amounts of sensitive and critical data within their Storage Area Networks (SANs), it becomes increasingly important to adhere to various compliance and regulatory requirements. Data security and privacy are at the forefront of modern enterprise IT strategies, and failure to meet legal and industry-specific standards can lead to substantial financial penalties, reputational damage, and operational disruptions. SAN environments, with their centralized and high-performance storage infrastructure, must align with these requirements to ensure that data is protected, accessible, and managed in compliance with applicable laws and standards. Understanding the complexities of compliance and regulatory requirements in SAN environments is essential for businesses that need to meet stringent obligations, safeguard sensitive information, and mitigate risks associated with non-compliance.

Compliance requirements vary widely depending on the industry, geographic location, and type of data being stored. For example, healthcare organizations must adhere to regulations such as the Health Insurance Portability and Accountability Act (HIPAA) in the United States, which mandates stringent protections for patient health data. Similarly, financial institutions must comply with the Sarbanes-Oxley Act (SOX), which requires secure data retention and auditing practices for financial records. Additionally, the General Data Protection Regulation (GDPR) has set new standards for the handling of personal data in the European Union, placing the responsibility on businesses to ensure that data is collected, stored, and processed with the utmost care and transparency. For any SAN environment, understanding the specific compliance frameworks that apply to the organization's operations is crucial to designing and managing the storage infrastructure.

One of the most significant challenges in SAN compliance is ensuring that data is properly secured. Many regulatory frameworks mandate that organizations take appropriate measures to protect sensitive data from unauthorized access, theft, or loss. Fiber Channel SANs, with their dedicated and high-speed infrastructure, are inherently more secure than IP-based storage networks because they operate in isolated, private networks. However, this does not eliminate the need for additional security measures such as encryption, access controls, and authentication mechanisms to ensure that data is protected both during transit and at rest. Encryption is particularly important for meeting regulatory requirements, as it ensures that data remains confidential even if it is intercepted. Many SANs are equipped with built-in encryption capabilities, but businesses must also consider whether their encryption standards align with regulatory guidelines, ensuring that strong encryption algorithms and key management practices are implemented.

Access control and authentication are other critical aspects of ensuring compliance in SAN environments. Regulatory standards often require that only authorized personnel have access to sensitive data. SANs typically implement zoning, which allows administrators to segment the network into smaller, isolated sections where only specific devices can communicate with each other. This helps prevent unauthorized access to sensitive data and ensures that only the necessary personnel and devices are granted access to specific resources. Additionally, SAN environments must enforce strict authentication protocols, such as multifactor authentication (MFA), to validate user identities before granting access to storage resources. By implementing robust access controls and authentication mechanisms, organizations can safeguard their data and meet compliance requirements that mandate strict user access policies.

Data retention is another important aspect of compliance in SAN environments. Many regulatory frameworks require that data be retained for a specified period, which can vary depending on the type of data and the industry. For example, financial records may need to be kept for several years to comply with SOX regulations, while healthcare data must be retained for a minimum period under HIPAA. In a SAN environment, businesses must ensure that data retention policies are implemented and adhered to by configuring storage resources to store data for the required duration. Retention policies should be automated to ensure consistency and prevent accidental data deletion. Additionally, businesses must ensure that deleted data is properly erased, so it cannot be recovered. This is particularly important for industries with stringent privacy laws, such as the GDPR, which mandates that data be deleted once it is no longer needed for the purpose for which it was collected.

Auditing and logging are also crucial components of compliance within SAN environments. Regulatory standards often require that organizations maintain an audit trail of data access and modification activities to ensure accountability and traceability. In a SAN environment, administrators must implement comprehensive logging mechanisms that track all user and system interactions with storage resources. These logs should include details such as who accessed data, what actions were taken, when the actions occurred, and whether any anomalies or unauthorized access attempts were detected. The ability to generate and review audit logs is essential for organizations to demonstrate compliance during regulatory audits and to detect any potential security breaches or violations. Additionally, logs must be protected to ensure that they cannot be tampered with, and they should be stored in a secure and compliant manner.

For businesses operating in multiple geographic regions, compliance with international data protection regulations can be particularly challenging. The GDPR, for instance, applies to organizations that handle the personal data of EU citizens, regardless of where the organization is based. This creates complexity for organizations with global operations, as they must ensure that their SAN environments adhere to local data privacy laws in each jurisdiction. One key aspect of the GDPR is the requirement to store and process personal data within the EU or in countries that meet the GDPR's data protection standards. This means that organizations may need to implement regional data storage strategies and ensure that their SAN infrastructure is configured to store and access data in compliance with these regulations. Organizations must also consider the implications of cross-border data transfers, which are subject to strict regulations under the GDPR and other data protection laws.

Cloud integration is another area where compliance and regulatory requirements must be carefully considered in SAN environments. As more businesses adopt hybrid cloud architectures, integrating on-premise SANs with cloud storage solutions becomes increasingly common. However, cloud storage presents unique challenges for compliance, particularly when it comes to data sovereignty and jurisdictional concerns. Organizations must ensure that their cloud service providers comply with relevant regulations, and that sensitive data is stored and processed in accordance with local laws. When integrating SAN environments with the cloud, businesses must ensure that encryption, access controls, and data retention policies are applied consistently across both on-premise and cloud storage resources. This requires careful planning and coordination to ensure that cloud-based storage is compliant with the same standards as on-premise SAN infrastructure.

Finally, businesses must stay up-to-date with evolving compliance requirements to ensure ongoing regulatory adherence. Regulatory frameworks are continuously evolving to address new threats and challenges in data security and privacy. For instance, recent updates to the GDPR have introduced stricter requirements for data access, consent, and portability, and similar changes are occurring in other regions. Organizations must monitor these changes and adapt their SAN environments and data protection strategies accordingly. Regular training for IT staff, the use of compliance management tools, and periodic audits can help ensure that the SAN infrastructure remains in alignment with current regulatory standards.

Navigating the complex landscape of compliance and regulatory requirements in SAN environments requires a thorough understanding of the relevant laws and standards, as well as a proactive approach to data management and security. By implementing strong security measures, access controls, retention policies, auditing mechanisms, and cloud integration strategies, organizations can ensure that their SAN environments meet regulatory requirements while protecting sensitive data and maintaining business continuity. Compliance is not just about meeting legal obligations—it is about building trust with customers, safeguarding business assets, and fostering a culture of responsibility in data management.

# Storage Tiering and Cost Optimization in Fiber Channel SANs

As organizations continue to generate vast amounts of data, the need for efficient storage management becomes increasingly important. Fiber Channel Storage Area Networks (SANs) are among the most popular solutions for high-performance, enterprise-level storage, providing a dedicated and high-speed network for data storage and retrieval. However, managing the growing volumes of data within a Fiber Channel SAN can be complex and costly. One effective way to optimize storage usage and reduce costs is through the implementation of storage tiering. Storage tiering allows organizations to classify data based on its value and frequency of access and store it across different types of storage media. By doing so, businesses can optimize both their storage resources and operational costs, ensuring that high-priority data is stored on the fastest, most expensive media, while less critical data is stored on slower, more cost-effective media.

Storage tiering involves organizing storage into different "tiers" that are assigned based on the performance needs of the data being stored. These tiers are often categorized by the speed and cost of the storage media, with higher-performing storage devices being more expensive. Typically, the highest-performing storage tiers consist of solid-state drives (SSDs) or high-speed fiber channel disk arrays, while lower tiers are made up of traditional hard disk drives (HDDs) or other more cost-effective storage media. The goal is to ensure that data is stored in a way that meets the performance requirements without wasting resources. For example, mission-critical data that is frequently accessed, such as transactional data in banking or real-time data in e-commerce, should be placed on the highest-performing storage tier to ensure quick access times. On the other hand, less frequently accessed data, such as archived records or infrequently used backup files, can be moved to lower-cost, slower storage tiers.

In Fiber Channel SANs, the ability to implement storage tiering provides several advantages. First and foremost, it enables businesses to optimize storage costs. High-performance storage media, such as SSDs, can be significantly more expensive than traditional HDDs. By storing only the most critical data on these high-performing devices, organizations can minimize their expenditure on expensive storage while still ensuring that the data that matters most is accessible with the speed and efficiency required. Conversely, less frequently used data can be offloaded to more cost-effective storage solutions, reducing the overall cost of the storage infrastructure without sacrificing performance for less critical applications.

Another benefit of storage tiering is improved resource utilization. With the large amounts of data that businesses generate today, it is essential to ensure that storage resources are used efficiently. Without tiering, organizations might store all data on high-performance storage systems, which could lead to inefficient use of both space and cost. With tiering, however, data is dynamically allocated to the appropriate storage tier based on its usage patterns, meaning that expensive high-performance resources are reserved for critical applications, while less demanding workloads are handled by more economical storage devices. This efficient allocation helps to avoid both over-provisioning and underutilization of storage resources, ensuring that the organization's infrastructure is running at its best.

Storage tiering also contributes to the overall performance of the Fiber Channel SAN. By segregating data according to its access frequency, businesses can ensure that high-priority data can be accessed quickly and efficiently. The placement of high-performance data on faster SSDs or high-speed Fiber Channel storage ensures that important workloads, such as real-time analytics, database queries, or online transactions, do not experience delays or bottlenecks. In contrast, storing less critical data on slower media ensures that these resources do not compete for bandwidth or system resources with more demanding applications. This segmentation of data allows for better load balancing within the SAN, enabling it to handle workloads more effectively and without unnecessary performance degradation.

One of the most significant challenges in implementing storage tiering in Fiber Channel SANs is managing the complexity of data movement across different tiers. As data usage patterns change over time, it may be necessary to migrate data between storage tiers to ensure that it remains in the most appropriate location. For example, data that was initially deemed highly critical and stored on a fast SSD might later be classified as less critical due to changes in business needs or access patterns. In these cases, automated data migration tools become crucial in ensuring that data is continuously moved to the appropriate tier based on its current importance or usage frequency. These tools can monitor the access frequency of data and automatically migrate it to the appropriate storage tier without requiring manual intervention, thus ensuring that storage resources are always allocated in the most cost-effective and efficient manner.

The ability to manage and optimize data movement between tiers requires robust software tools and policies that help automate the tiering process. These tools typically rely on algorithms that classify data based on access frequency, age, or other relevant metrics. The management software can identify hot, warm, and cold data, and automatically assign it to the appropriate storage tier. Hot data, which is accessed frequently and requires fast access times, is typically moved to high-performance storage. Warm data, which is accessed intermittently, may be placed on mid-tier storage solutions, while cold data, which is rarely accessed, can be moved to low-cost, long-term storage. This automated tiering process helps organizations maintain an efficient and cost-effective SAN environment, reducing the need for constant manual intervention.

Data security is another important factor in storage tiering, especially as it relates to cost optimization. While moving data to lower-cost storage tiers can save money, it is essential to ensure that the security measures applied to higher-tier storage are equally effective for lower-tier storage. Sensitive data, such as customer information or financial records, must be protected regardless of where it is stored. This means implementing encryption, access control policies, and regular audits across all storage tiers to ensure that data remains secure, even when it is stored on less expensive media. As data is moved between tiers, it is important to ensure that these security measures are maintained, so businesses can comply with regulatory requirements and prevent unauthorized access to sensitive information.

In addition to cost savings, storage tiering also enables better disaster recovery capabilities. With a multi-tiered storage architecture, organizations can ensure that critical data is backed up on high-speed, reliable storage systems, while less critical data is stored on less expensive, slower devices. In the event of a disaster, organizations can quickly restore high-priority data from high-performance storage, while more time-consuming restoration processes can be applied to lower-priority data from more economical storage tiers. This tiered approach to disaster recovery helps to ensure that business-critical data is recovered quickly, minimizing downtime and ensuring business continuity.

Finally, as businesses move toward hybrid cloud environments, the ability to integrate storage tiering between on-premise SANs and cloud storage solutions becomes increasingly important. Cloud storage offers scalable, cost-effective options for long-term or archival data, while Fiber Channel SANs provide fast and reliable access for high-priority applications. By implementing a tiered storage strategy that spans both on-premise and cloud environments, organizations can optimize their storage costs and ensure that their data is always available in the most appropriate location, based on its value and access needs.

The implementation of storage tiering in Fiber Channel SANs offers numerous benefits, including cost optimization, improved performance, better resource utilization, and more efficient disaster recovery strategies. By dynamically managing data placement across different storage tiers, businesses can ensure that their storage infrastructure is both cost-effective and highly performant. This approach also supports scalability, enabling organizations to grow their storage environments without compromising efficiency or performance. With the right tools and policies in place, organizations can take full advantage of storage tiering to optimize their Fiber Channel SANs for both cost and performance, positioning themselves for success in an increasingly data-driven world.

# Energy Efficiency and Green Storage Solutions in SANs

As the demand for data storage continues to grow exponentially, organizations are increasingly focusing on the environmental impact of their data centers. The need for energy efficiency and sustainability in Storage Area Networks (SANs) has never been more pressing. SANs, with their high-performance storage infrastructure, consume significant amounts of power, contributing to the overall carbon footprint of an organization's IT operations. In response to this challenge, businesses are adopting green storage solutions and energy-efficient technologies to optimize their SAN environments, reduce energy consumption, and meet sustainability goals. The transition to more energy-efficient SANs is not only an environmentally responsible choice but also a cost-effective strategy for businesses looking to manage their operational expenses and improve overall efficiency.

One of the most significant factors driving the adoption of green storage solutions in SAN environments is the increasing energy consumption of data centers. As organizations store more data, the infrastructure required to support that data must expand, leading to higher energy usage. SANs, which provide centralized storage for enterprise applications and critical data, require substantial power to operate, especially when the SAN architecture involves multiple

171

storage arrays, switches, and servers. The cooling systems needed to maintain the optimal temperature for these systems also add to the overall energy demand. As a result, data centers that utilize traditional storage technologies can face significant energy costs, particularly as storage capacities increase. Energy-efficient SAN solutions help mitigate these costs by reducing the amount of power needed to run and maintain storage infrastructure, contributing to both lower operational expenses and a smaller carbon footprint.

One approach to improving energy efficiency in SANs is by optimizing the utilization of storage resources through better management of power consumption. Many modern storage devices, such as solid-state drives (SSDs) and high-density hard disk drives (HDDs), include built-in power management features that automatically adjust power consumption based on usage patterns. For example, when storage devices are not actively in use, they can enter low-power states, reducing the energy required to operate them. Additionally, by consolidating storage devices into a smaller number of more efficient systems, organizations can reduce the number of devices that require constant power, further minimizing energy usage. This practice, often referred to as storage consolidation, helps organizations balance performance and energy efficiency, ensuring that only the necessary storage devices are active at any given time.

Another key strategy for improving energy efficiency in SANs is to implement storage tiering. Storage tiering involves categorizing data based on its importance and frequency of access and placing it on different types of storage media accordingly. Critical, high-performance data is placed on fast, energy-intensive devices such as SSDs, while less critical data is stored on slower, more energy-efficient media like traditional HDDs or tape. By aligning storage resources with the specific needs of the data, organizations can reduce the energy consumption associated with unnecessary high-performance storage while ensuring that data is still accessible when needed. This approach not only optimizes energy use but also ensures that performance requirements are met without over-provisioning energy-demanding storage solutions.

Data deduplication and compression technologies are also becoming integral to green storage solutions in SAN environments. These technologies reduce the amount of data that needs to be stored by eliminating duplicate copies and compressing data to make more efficient use of available storage space. The reduction in data volume directly leads to a decrease in the storage resources needed, which in turn lowers the energy consumption of the SAN. With less data to store and manage, organizations can reduce the number of active storage devices, resulting in significant energy savings. Furthermore, the reduced data footprint enables better resource utilization, allowing organizations to store more data on fewer, more energy-efficient devices.

In addition to optimizing the storage hardware, organizations are also investing in more energy-efficient network infrastructure for their SANs. Fiber Channel SANs, known for their high-speed connectivity and reliability, can also be optimized for energy efficiency. For instance, modern Fiber Channel switches are designed with energy-saving features, such as low-power modes and efficient power supply units, that reduce overall energy consumption. By upgrading to newer, more energy-efficient switches and components, organizations can significantly reduce the energy required to operate their SAN networks. Furthermore, using software-defined storage (SDS) solutions in conjunction with Fiber Channel SANs can help optimize the flow of data across the network, reducing unnecessary energy expenditure on network resources.

Cooling is another area where significant energy savings can be achieved. Data centers housing SANs require powerful cooling systems to maintain an optimal operating temperature for the equipment. These systems, particularly in large-scale environments, can consume a considerable amount of energy. To mitigate this, organizations are increasingly adopting more efficient cooling techniques, such as hot aisle/cold aisle configurations, liquid cooling, and free cooling solutions. By improving the overall thermal management in the data center, organizations can reduce the amount of energy required to maintain a consistent temperature, thus lowering the total energy consumption of the SAN infrastructure.

The integration of renewable energy sources into data center operations is another important trend in the quest for more sustainable SAN environments. As organizations aim to reduce their carbon footprint and become more environmentally responsible, many are exploring the use of renewable energy sources, such as solar, wind, and hydroelectric power, to power their data centers. By investing in renewable energy, businesses can reduce their dependence on traditional, carbon-intensive power sources, further minimizing their environmental impact. Moreover, some data centers are located in regions where renewable energy is abundant and cost-effective, making it a viable and attractive option for organizations looking to operate more sustainably.

Energy-efficient SAN solutions also support sustainability reporting and compliance with environmental regulations. Many organizations are subject to various national and international regulations that require them to report their energy usage and demonstrate their commitment to sustainability. Implementing energy-efficient SAN technologies helps organizations meet these regulatory requirements while also contributing to broader environmental goals. For example, the Energy Star certification program recognizes products and systems that meet high energy efficiency standards, and organizations can achieve this certification by adopting energy-efficient SAN solutions. By aligning with these standards, businesses can demonstrate their commitment to environmental responsibility, enhance their brand reputation, and potentially benefit from incentives or tax breaks associated with sustainable operations.

As the demand for data storage continues to rise, it is essential for businesses to prioritize energy efficiency in their SAN environments. The integration of energy-efficient storage hardware, optimized data management practices, and sustainable cooling and energy sourcing strategies can help reduce energy consumption, lower operational costs, and support environmental sustainability. By embracing green storage solutions, businesses not only reduce their carbon footprint but also improve the overall efficiency and performance of their data centers. As energy efficiency becomes a key factor in the design and management of SANs, organizations are positioned to achieve long-term cost savings while contributing to the global effort to reduce environmental impact.

# Evaluating and Selecting Fiber Channel SAN Vendors

Selecting the right Fiber Channel Storage Area Network (SAN) vendor is a crucial decision for any organization looking to build or upgrade their data storage infrastructure. A well-chosen vendor not only provides the hardware and software necessary to establish a reliable and high-performance SAN but also offers ongoing support, scalability, and integration capabilities that align with an organization's unique needs. Given the wide range of vendors and solutions available in the market, evaluating and selecting the most appropriate vendor requires careful consideration of multiple factors, including performance, reliability, scalability, cost, support services, and future growth potential. This decision will impact the efficiency and effectiveness of the entire data storage environment, making it essential to approach the selection process with a thorough and systematic methodology.

One of the first considerations when evaluating Fiber Channel SAN vendors is performance. The primary function of a SAN is to provide fast, reliable access to large volumes of data. Different vendors offer varying levels of performance based on the quality of their hardware and the capabilities of their software. When assessing performance, it is important to evaluate the throughput, latency, and overall speed of the solution. Vendors may offer different speeds for their Fiber Channel products, such as 8Gbps, 16Gbps, and 32Gbps, with higher speeds typically delivering faster data transfer rates. Organizations must carefully assess their data transfer needs, considering factors such as the size of their datasets, the speed of access required for different applications, and whether they are dealing with high-throughput applications such as big data analytics or real-time processing. The vendor's ability to offer high-speed solutions that meet these requirements should be a key part of the evaluation process.

In addition to raw performance, reliability is a critical factor in selecting a Fiber Channel SAN vendor. Data availability and fault tolerance are central to the functionality of a SAN, as downtime or data loss can have serious consequences for business operations. A reliable SAN should provide built-in redundancy features, such as dual controllers, failover mechanisms, and multipathing capabilities, to ensure that the system remains operational even if one component fails. Vendors that offer robust reliability features such as hot-swappable components, automatic failover, and load balancing across multiple paths will typically be more desirable than those with less resilient systems. Organizations should also assess the vendor's track record in delivering high-availability solutions and review customer feedback to understand the real-world reliability of their SAN solutions.

Scalability is another essential factor when evaluating Fiber Channel SAN vendors. As data storage needs evolve and grow over time, the chosen SAN must be able to scale to accommodate increasing volumes of data and users. The vendor's ability to provide scalable solutions that grow with an organization's requirements is vital. A good Fiber Channel SAN solution should allow for easy expansion, whether through adding more storage devices, increasing network bandwidth, or extending the SAN to additional locations. Organizations must consider not only current storage needs but also anticipate future growth, including increased data storage, higher performance demands, and expanding workloads. Vendors that offer modular, flexible solutions are typically better suited for businesses planning for long-term growth and evolving storage requirements.

Cost is always a significant consideration when selecting any technology solution, including Fiber Channel SANs. The initial cost of the hardware and software, along with ongoing operational and maintenance costs, should be carefully evaluated. While it may be tempting to choose the least expensive solution, it is essential to weigh the total cost of ownership (TCO) over the long term. Cheaper SAN solutions may have higher operational costs in terms of power consumption, maintenance, or scalability limitations, which could lead to higher total costs down the line. Conversely, a higher-priced solution might offer better performance, reliability, and scalability, providing greater value in the long run. Organizations should consider not only the upfront costs but also the anticipated operating expenses, including power consumption, system upgrades, and the cost of managing and supporting the system.

Support and service offerings are crucial when evaluating vendors. A Fiber Channel SAN is a complex system that requires ongoing support and maintenance to ensure optimal performance. The vendor's ability to provide timely, effective support can be the deciding factor in ensuring the success of the SAN implementation. Vendors typically offer different levels of support, including 24/7 technical assistance, software updates, hardware warranties, and on-site support for system failures. The quality of the vendor's customer service, as well as the availability and responsiveness of their support team, should be carefully considered. Organizations should also investigate whether the vendor offers training and educational resources to help internal staff manage and troubleshoot the SAN effectively. The vendor's reputation for customer service can provide insight into the overall reliability and user-friendliness of the product.

Another key consideration when evaluating Fiber Channel SAN vendors is the vendor's ecosystem and compatibility with existing IT infrastructure. It is essential that the SAN solution integrates well with other systems and technologies already in place, such as servers, networking hardware, and backup solutions. Compatibility with different operating systems and virtualization platforms, as well as ease of integration with existing storage management software, can significantly impact the success of the SAN deployment. Vendors that offer solutions that are compatible with a wide range of third-party applications and systems provide more flexibility and can minimize the risk of compatibility issues. Additionally, organizations should consider how easily the SAN solution can be integrated with cloud services or hybrid cloud environments, as many businesses are increasingly adopting cloud storage alongside on-premise solutions.

Security is a growing concern in today's data storage environment, and evaluating a vendor's security features is a critical part of the selection process. Fiber Channel SANs are inherently more secure than traditional IP-based storage networks due to their isolated nature, but additional security features, such as encryption, authentication, and access control, are often required to meet regulatory compliance standards. Vendors should offer robust security features that allow organizations to protect sensitive data from unauthorized access, loss, or theft. These features may include data encryption both at rest and in transit, role-based access control, and secure remote management capabilities. Organizations should also investigate whether the vendor offers auditing and logging capabilities to track access and modifications to critical data.

Finally, organizations should assess the vendor's commitment to future innovation and the long-term viability of their solutions. The technology landscape is constantly evolving, and businesses need to ensure that the vendor they select will continue to offer updates, new features, and solutions that meet future demands. This can be assessed by reviewing the vendor's roadmap for product development, their participation in industry standards and initiatives, and their ability to adopt emerging technologies, such as NVMe over Fiber Channel, for high-performance storage environments. A vendor that is committed to staying at the forefront of technology will help ensure that the SAN solution remains viable and relevant for years to come.

Choosing the right Fiber Channel SAN vendor is a multifaceted decision that requires evaluating performance, reliability, scalability, cost, support, security, and future innovation. By thoroughly assessing these factors, organizations can select a vendor that aligns with their current and future storage needs, ensuring the successful deployment and operation of their SAN infrastructure. With the right vendor partnership, businesses can establish a SAN environment that delivers high performance, seamless integration, and long-term value.

# Fiber Channel SAN Testing and Validation Procedures

Testing and validating a Fiber Channel Storage Area Network (SAN) are essential steps in ensuring that the system operates at optimal performance and meets the organization's data management and storage needs. As organizations increasingly rely on high-speed, high-performance storage solutions, a failure in the SAN can have severe consequences, including data unavailability, system downtime, and potential financial loss. Therefore, robust testing and validation procedures are necessary to ensure that the SAN infrastructure is reliable, secure, and scalable. These procedures should focus on various aspects of the SAN, including performance, connectivity, security, and disaster recovery, to verify that all components are functioning as intended and can handle the demands placed on them.

One of the primary objectives of testing a Fiber Channel SAN is to validate its performance. The SAN is expected to deliver high throughput and low latency for critical data applications, and performance testing ensures that these expectations are met. To evaluate performance, administrators should conduct throughput and latency tests under various loads and configurations. Throughput testing involves measuring the amount of data the SAN can transfer in a given period, while latency testing assesses how quickly data can be accessed or written. These tests can be conducted using benchmark tools that simulate real-world workloads, providing insights into the system's ability to handle the expected data volumes. During testing, it is crucial to examine both the network and storage devices to ensure that the entire system, from the switches to the storage arrays, can maintain high performance. Performance testing should also cover different configurations, such as the use of different Fiber Channel speeds, ensuring that the SAN can meet varying demands.

In addition to performance, connectivity is another critical area that requires testing and validation. Since a Fiber Channel SAN is a networked environment, ensuring that all devices can communicate seamlessly across the network is paramount. Connectivity testing should verify that all components, such as servers, storage devices, and switches, can establish stable, reliable connections. This involves testing each device in isolation and as part of the overall network to identify potential connectivity issues. For instance, devices should be tested for their ability to establish connections when powered on, verify that the correct zoning configurations are in place, and ensure that failover mechanisms work effectively in case of a network link failure. Furthermore, administrators should test multipathing configurations to ensure that multiple data paths are functioning correctly and that traffic is being load-balanced effectively across the network. This process helps prevent bottlenecks and ensures the network can recover from failures without disrupting data access.

Security is also a crucial aspect of SAN testing and validation. Fiber Channel networks are typically used to store sensitive, mission-critical data, and ensuring the security of the SAN infrastructure is paramount.

Security testing should include validating access control mechanisms, such as zoning and authentication policies, to ensure that only authorized devices can access the SAN and its data. This involves reviewing the zoning configurations and ensuring that devices are isolated appropriately, preventing unauthorized devices from communicating with sensitive data. Additionally, testing authentication methods, such as port-based security or challenge-response authentication, ensures that only authorized users or devices can connect to the SAN. Encryption is another key security feature that must be tested. Both in-transit and at-rest data encryption should be validated to ensure that data is protected against unauthorized access or breaches. Administrators should also conduct vulnerability assessments to identify and address potential security gaps, such as unpatched vulnerabilities or weak configurations.

Disaster recovery and data integrity testing are also essential components of the SAN validation process. A Fiber Channel SAN must support business continuity and disaster recovery requirements by ensuring that data can be recovered quickly and reliably in case of failure. Validation should include testing the SAN's backup and restore procedures, such as ensuring that data can be consistently replicated to remote locations and recovered without data loss. Testing replication between primary and secondary storage systems, as well as failover between active and passive storage devices, ensures that the SAN can function effectively during disruptions. Simulating scenarios such as hardware failure or network outages can help verify the robustness of these recovery mechanisms. For instance, administrators can simulate a disk failure and verify that the SAN can continue to function using redundant devices or paths, maintaining high availability and minimizing downtime. It is also crucial to test the restore process, ensuring that backup data can be restored to the correct point in time, particularly when dealing with large datasets or time-sensitive information.

Furthermore, organizations must validate the scalability of their Fiber Channel SAN infrastructure. As businesses grow, the SAN must be capable of expanding to meet increased storage and performance demands. Scalability testing should focus on adding new storage devices or servers to the SAN and verifying that they integrate seamlessly with the existing infrastructure. This includes testing the

SAN's ability to handle increased traffic, such as adding additional users, virtual machines, or data streams, and ensuring that performance remains stable under higher loads. Scalability testing also involves testing the upgradeability of the system, including firmware updates and hardware replacements. By simulating an increase in capacity and performance needs, administrators can ensure that the SAN can scale without causing performance degradation or downtime.

Additionally, thorough testing should ensure that the SAN can handle various workloads without compromising its performance or reliability. Workload testing involves simulating different types of data access patterns, such as random read/write, sequential read/write, and mixed workloads, to evaluate how the SAN performs under different conditions. These tests can identify potential areas of weakness in the SAN infrastructure and help administrators optimize the system for specific use cases. It is essential to simulate the expected real-world conditions of the SAN, such as high-concurrency environments or data-intensive applications, to validate that the system can manage these demands effectively.

Finally, testing should include validating the monitoring and management capabilities of the SAN system. Effective monitoring tools are essential for identifying potential issues before they become critical problems. Testing the SAN's monitoring tools should include verifying the system's ability to capture and report performance metrics, network traffic, storage utilization, and device health in real-time. This allows administrators to quickly identify performance bottlenecks, potential hardware failures, or configuration issues. Additionally, testing the management interfaces ensures that administrators can efficiently manage the SAN, configure devices, and make changes to zoning, storage allocation, or security policies without encountering difficulties.

The testing and validation of a Fiber Channel SAN are fundamental steps to ensuring the system performs as expected, provides high availability, and meets business continuity requirements. By addressing performance, connectivity, security, disaster recovery, scalability, and management, organizations can ensure that their SAN infrastructure is reliable, efficient, and capable of supporting their data storage and access needs. Proper testing not only helps identify potential issues before they impact operations but also ensures that the SAN will continue to perform effectively as the organization's storage needs evolve over time. By thoroughly validating the SAN environment, businesses can confidently rely on their infrastructure to meet the challenges of modern data management.

# Building a Scalable Fiber Channel SAN Architecture

Building a scalable Fiber Channel Storage Area Network (SAN) architecture is a critical task for organizations that need to ensure their data storage infrastructure can grow with the business while maintaining high performance, reliability, and availability. The core idea behind scalability in a SAN is to design an architecture that not only meets the current storage and performance needs but also accommodates future growth without requiring significant redesigns or disruptions. A well-designed scalable Fiber Channel SAN provides the flexibility to expand storage capacity, increase data throughput, and improve overall system performance as data demands increase. To achieve this, a deep understanding of the organization's current and future storage needs, along with best practices in SAN design, is essential.

The foundation of a scalable Fiber Channel SAN begins with selecting the right components that will allow for expansion as business needs grow. The primary components of a Fiber Channel SAN include the host bus adapters (HBAs), switches, storage devices, and the underlying fiber optic infrastructure. Each of these components must be selected not only for their ability to meet current requirements but also for their scalability and flexibility in future-proofing the SAN. For example, when selecting Fiber Channel switches, it is important to choose models that support higher speeds (e.g., 16Gbps, 32Gbps) and have the ability to add additional ports or extend the network as needed. Fiber Channel switches that allow for non-disruptive expansion ensure that as new devices or storage arrays are added, the SAN can accommodate the increased load without performance degradation or system downtime.

Another key consideration in building a scalable SAN is the network design itself. Fiber Channel SANs are typically built using a fabric topology, where switches interconnect storage devices and hosts. The fabric topology provides redundancy, high availability, and scalability, as it allows devices to communicate across multiple paths. To scale effectively, a SAN must support high-bandwidth connections and be capable of routing data across different paths in the event of a failure. This means choosing switches and network components that support multipathing, allowing data traffic to be rerouted dynamically to avoid congested or failed links. By planning for multiple paths between devices, the network can continue to operate efficiently even as it grows, minimizing the risk of downtime and ensuring uninterrupted data access.

In addition to the physical network topology, managing the zoning within the Fiber Channel SAN is another critical aspect of scalability. Zoning is the process of logically grouping devices within the SAN to control access between them. By implementing a well-organized zoning strategy, administrators can ensure that new devices can be added without disrupting existing configurations. It also helps maintain the security and integrity of the network by controlling which devices are allowed to communicate with one another. As the SAN grows, zoning can be dynamically adjusted to accommodate new storage arrays, servers, and other devices. Using zoning effectively helps prevent unnecessary broadcast traffic, minimizes the risk of configuration errors, and allows for the isolation of specific devices or storage resources as needed.

Scalability in a Fiber Channel SAN is also dependent on the capacity and performance of the storage arrays themselves. As the volume of data grows, organizations need to ensure that their storage infrastructure can handle the increased workload. When selecting storage arrays for scalability, it is important to choose devices that support high-density configurations, allowing more storage to be added without requiring additional physical space. Additionally, storage arrays should be capable of supporting different types of storage media, such as solid-state drives (SSDs) and hard disk drives (HDDs), to balance performance and cost. Hybrid arrays that combine both SSDs and HDDs allow organizations to store high-performance data on faster SSDs while archiving less frequently accessed data on slower, cost-effective HDDs. This tiered storage approach ensures that storage resources are utilized efficiently as the SAN scales, without overwhelming the system with high-performance data that could be placed on slower media.

One of the most important factors in building a scalable Fiber Channel SAN is ensuring the infrastructure supports ease of expansion. The system should be able to add new devices or storage arrays without causing disruptions to the existing configuration. This can be achieved by implementing modular components that can be easily upgraded or added to the existing infrastructure. For example, using modular switches that support additional ports or fabric expansion can allow the SAN to grow organically as new devices or servers are added. This modular approach provides flexibility and minimizes the need for costly and disruptive overhauls. Additionally, the use of virtualized storage and software-defined storage (SDS) platforms can help abstract the underlying hardware, making it easier to scale the SAN and integrate with new technologies.

Automation also plays a key role in managing a scalable Fiber Channel SAN. As the SAN grows, manually configuring, managing, and monitoring the system becomes increasingly difficult and prone to error. Automation tools can help streamline these tasks by enabling automatic provisioning of storage resources, dynamic path management, and real-time monitoring. By automating routine tasks, administrators can focus on more strategic aspects of SAN management, such as performance tuning and resource optimization. Automation also ensures that new devices are automatically configured to integrate with the existing infrastructure, reducing the chances of configuration errors and improving overall system reliability.

When designing a scalable SAN, it is also essential to consider the future of storage technologies. The landscape of data storage is rapidly evolving, with technologies such as NVMe over Fiber Channel (NVMe-oF) and non-volatile memory (NVM) providing significant improvements in speed and performance. A scalable SAN architecture should be able to integrate with these emerging technologies without requiring a complete redesign. Ensuring that the SAN is compatible with next-generation storage solutions allows organizations to keep pace with technological advancements and future-proof their infrastructure. By selecting hardware and software that can be easily upgraded to support emerging storage technologies, businesses can extend the lifespan of their SAN while maintaining high performance and reliability.

Security is another vital aspect of building a scalable SAN architecture. As the SAN grows and becomes more complex, ensuring the security of the data and the network itself becomes increasingly important. Fiber Channel SANs are typically more secure than traditional IP-based storage networks due to their isolated nature, but additional security measures, such as encryption and access control, are necessary to protect sensitive data. A scalable SAN must include robust security features that can be expanded as the system grows. This includes implementing encryption at rest and in transit, using role-based access control (RBAC) for managing user privileges, and ensuring that zoning policies are properly configured to restrict unauthorized access.

Finally, managing the cost of scaling the SAN is a key consideration. Although scalability allows for future growth, it also requires careful planning to avoid excessive costs. Businesses should plan for incremental growth, adding capacity and performance as needed rather than overbuilding the system upfront. This approach helps ensure that the SAN remains cost-effective and avoids unnecessary expenses associated with underutilized infrastructure. By balancing performance requirements with cost considerations, organizations can create a scalable Fiber Channel SAN that meets both their current and future needs while maintaining budgetary control.

Building a scalable Fiber Channel SAN architecture requires a thoughtful, strategic approach that balances performance, reliability, security, and cost. By selecting the right components, designing an efficient network topology, and ensuring ease of expansion, businesses can create a SAN that can grow and adapt to evolving data storage requirements. With careful planning and the use of modular, flexible solutions, organizations can build a SAN infrastructure that supports their long-term data management goals while minimizing the risk of performance bottlenecks or costly system upgrades.

# Interoperability Challenges in Fiber Channel Networks

Fiber Channel networks are widely recognized for their high-performance, low-latency, and high-availability features, making them an essential component of many enterprise data centers. However, despite these advantages, one of the most significant challenges organizations face when implementing and managing Fiber Channel SANs (Storage Area Networks) is interoperability. Interoperability refers to the ability of various hardware and software components from different vendors to work seamlessly together within the same network environment. In the context of Fiber Channel networks, ensuring that devices such as switches, storage arrays, host bus adapters (HBAs), and cables from different manufacturers can communicate effectively is critical for maintaining a reliable and scalable storage infrastructure. Unfortunately, achieving smooth interoperability between different components can be fraught with difficulties, ranging from compatibility issues to configuration conflicts, all of which can hinder the overall performance and reliability of the network.

One of the most common interoperability challenges in Fiber Channel networks stems from the variety of hardware and software products available on the market. Different vendors design their components to conform to the basic Fiber Channel standards, but variations in implementation can lead to compatibility issues. For example, different vendors may offer switches, HBAs, or storage arrays with slightly differing firmware or protocols, which can affect the ability of these components to communicate with each other. While Fiber Channel is an open standard, vendor-specific enhancements and optimizations can result in performance inconsistencies when components from different manufacturers are mixed in a single SAN. These variations can result in devices not recognizing each other, leading to connectivity failures, or in degraded performance when components do not work together as efficiently as they would with devices from the same vendor.

Another source of interoperability issues in Fiber Channel networks is the use of different generations of Fiber Channel technology. Over the years, Fiber Channel has evolved from earlier versions like 1Gbps and

2Gbps to more recent versions such as 8Gbps, 16Gbps, and 32Gbps. These advancements in speed, while improving network performance, introduce complexities when trying to integrate different generations of equipment into the same network. For instance, devices that support 8Gbps may not be backward compatible with those that support 16Gbps, and older equipment may not fully utilize the benefits of newer, faster Fiber Channel speeds. Furthermore, while newer devices are typically backward-compatible with older versions, the performance of the entire network can be limited to the speed of the slowest device in the network. This backward compatibility can introduce inefficiencies and bottlenecks, affecting the overall performance and throughput of the network.

Firmware mismatches are another significant challenge when dealing with interoperability in Fiber Channel networks. Each device in a Fiber Channel SAN, from switches to HBAs to storage devices, relies on firmware to manage communication, security, and data transfer processes. As vendors release firmware updates to improve performance, enhance security, or fix bugs, keeping all devices in the network synchronized becomes a complex task. Incompatibilities between firmware versions can lead to communication breakdowns, data corruption, or even network outages. For instance, a mismatch in firmware versions between a switch and an HBA may cause the HBA to fail to communicate with the switch, disrupting data transfers. Similarly, discrepancies between firmware versions on storage arrays and the network switches may lead to improper routing of data, increasing the risk of data loss or delays. To mitigate these issues, organizations must ensure that firmware updates are tested thoroughly across all components in the SAN before being deployed to avoid disrupting interoperability.

Another challenge that arises from interoperability concerns is the difficulty of managing multi-vendor environments. As businesses often purchase storage components from multiple vendors, managing a Fiber Channel SAN composed of equipment from various sources can become cumbersome. The challenge here lies in the management software, which may not be fully compatible with all devices in the SAN. SAN management software is responsible for monitoring the health of devices, configuring zoning, and ensuring that data flows efficiently across the network. However, if the software is designed to work optimally with equipment from one vendor but is tasked with managing devices from other vendors, the result can be a lack of cohesion and suboptimal management capabilities. Additionally, troubleshooting in a multi-vendor environment can be complex, as problems can arise from misconfigured components or from a lack of integration between the monitoring tools provided by different manufacturers. This can make it difficult for IT teams to identify the root cause of an issue when the system is not performing as expected.

Compatibility issues also extend to the cabling and connectors used in Fiber Channel SANs. While the basic design of Fiber Channel cabling, particularly fiber optic cables, follows industry standards, various vendors may use different types of cables, connectors, and transceivers that can cause incompatibility issues. Differences in cable quality, length, and connector types can introduce signal loss or degradation, leading to slower data transfer rates or even complete connection failures. Furthermore, when organizations are scaling their SANs, they may need to incorporate third-party cables and connectors, and ensuring that these components are fully compatible with the rest of the network can be a challenge. Fiber Channel networks require precise, high-quality cabling and connectors to function optimally, and any deviations in this infrastructure can lead to significant performance issues.

The complexity of integrating SAN environments with other types of storage networks, such as iSCSI or NFS, adds another layer of interoperability challenges. Many organizations operate hybrid environments that combine Fiber Channel SANs with other storage solutions for specific use cases. However, the differences between these storage technologies in terms of protocols, network configurations, and data handling can lead to integration difficulties. For example, the block-level storage approach of Fiber Channel SANs differs significantly from the file-level storage approach of NFS, and integrating these two systems requires careful planning to ensure data is transferred between the networks efficiently and without data loss. Moreover, ensuring that storage resources from different networks are properly allocated and accessed can require complex mapping and configuration processes.

In addressing these interoperability challenges, organizations must prioritize careful planning, testing, and ongoing maintenance. Thorough testing of all components before deployment is essential to ensure compatibility across the entire network. Additionally, organizations must implement standardized processes for updating firmware, managing multi-vendor environments, and maintaining the network infrastructure. The use of automation tools can help streamline the management of a multi-vendor SAN, as these tools can provide consistent monitoring and configuration across different devices and vendors. Moreover, collaboration with vendors to ensure compatibility and to obtain support for integration issues can help mitigate some of the difficulties that arise when operating a heterogeneous SAN environment.

Interoperability challenges in Fiber Channel networks are complex and can have significant consequences for network performance, reliability, and scalability. To build and maintain a high-functioning SAN, organizations must take a proactive approach to selecting compatible components, testing configurations, and managing a diverse infrastructure. By addressing these challenges head-on, businesses can ensure that their Fiber Channel SAN remains efficient, reliable, and capable of supporting their growing data storage needs.

# Implementing Fiber Channel Networks for SMBs

Implementing Fiber Channel networks in small and medium-sized businesses (SMBs) can be a highly effective way to improve data management and storage performance. While traditionally seen as a technology suited for large enterprises with extensive IT infrastructures, Fiber Channel networks are becoming increasingly accessible to SMBs as the costs of the necessary hardware and equipment have decreased over time. Fiber Channel offers significant advantages, including high-speed data transfer, low latency, and the ability to scale as the business grows. These features make Fiber Channel networks an ideal solution for SMBs that require reliable, high-performance storage solutions but do not have the resources to implement the more complex infrastructure used in larger organizations. However, implementing Fiber Channel networks in SMBs requires a careful approach to ensure that the solution is cost-effective, scalable, and meets the specific needs of the business.

The first step in implementing a Fiber Channel network in an SMB is determining whether Fiber Channel is the right solution for the business. Many SMBs rely on network-attached storage (NAS) or direct-attached storage (DAS) systems, which are generally simpler and more affordable alternatives to SANs. However, as data demands increase and businesses require faster, more reliable access to large volumes of data, these solutions can become limiting. Fiber Channel SANs provide high performance, high availability, and fault tolerance, making them ideal for businesses that need to access large amounts of data quickly and securely. When evaluating the need for a Fiber Channel network, SMBs should consider factors such as the volume of data they need to manage, the number of users accessing the data, and the performance requirements of the business-critical applications that rely on the storage system.

One of the key advantages of Fiber Channel is its ability to provide high-speed data transfers with low latency. For SMBs that rely on applications like databases, customer relationship management (CRM) systems, or data analytics tools, the speed at which data can be accessed and written is crucial. Fiber Channel operates over a dedicated network, allowing for faster and more efficient data transfer than typical Ethernet-based networks. This makes Fiber Channel a valuable solution for businesses that require fast access to their storage devices, especially as the volume of data grows. Fiber Channel's ability to scale with the business is another important factor for SMBs. As a business expands, its storage needs will also increase. Fiber Channel networks can easily accommodate growth, allowing SMBs to add new devices or expand their network without significant disruptions.

One of the challenges SMBs face when implementing Fiber Channel networks is the cost of the equipment. Fiber Channel switches, host bus adapters (HBAs), and storage arrays can be expensive, and SMBs may be concerned about the initial investment required to set up a SAN. However, the total cost of ownership can be lower over time, as Fiber Channel networks provide greater reliability, performance, and scalability than other storage solutions. Additionally, there are now more affordable Fiber Channel products on the market, making it easier for SMBs to implement SANs without the high upfront costs that were previously associated with this technology. Moreover, the improved efficiency and productivity offered by Fiber Channel SANs can lead to significant long-term savings, as businesses can access and manage their data more efficiently.

When planning the implementation of a Fiber Channel network, SMBs must also consider the infrastructure required to support the system. Fiber Channel networks require fiber optic cabling, which is generally more expensive than traditional copper cabling used in Ethernet networks. However, the higher performance and reliability of fiber optic connections make it an ideal choice for a high-speed SAN. SMBs should also consider the physical space needed for the network components. Fiber Channel switches and storage devices require dedicated space in a data center or server room, and the network needs to be designed to ensure proper airflow and cooling for the equipment. Proper planning of the infrastructure ensures that the SAN operates at peak performance and is capable of scaling with the business as it grows.

Security is another critical consideration when implementing Fiber Channel SANs for SMBs. Fiber Channel networks are typically more secure than Ethernet-based storage systems due to their isolated nature. Data transmitted over a Fiber Channel network does not travel over the same network as general internet or office traffic, making it less susceptible to unauthorized access or interception. However, additional security measures must be put in place to protect sensitive data and ensure compliance with any regulatory requirements. For SMBs, implementing zoning is an essential step in securing the SAN. Zoning allows administrators to restrict access between devices within the SAN, ensuring that only authorized devices can communicate with one another. Fiber Channel networks also support strong encryption, both at rest and in transit, to further enhance security. Ensuring that the SAN is properly secured is critical, particularly for SMBs that handle sensitive customer or financial data.

When selecting a Fiber Channel SAN solution for an SMB, businesses should consider the vendor's support and service offerings. Unlike larger organizations with dedicated IT teams, SMBs often rely on third-party support for their storage infrastructure. Therefore, it is important to select a vendor that offers comprehensive support, including installation, configuration, maintenance, and troubleshooting. A vendor with a strong support network can help SMBs address issues quickly and minimize downtime, which is crucial for maintaining business continuity. Many vendors also offer remote monitoring and management services, allowing SMBs to ensure that their SAN is functioning optimally without needing to dedicate full-time resources to the task. Additionally, SMBs should consider the ease of integration with existing IT systems, such as servers, backup solutions, and other network devices. A Fiber Channel SAN should integrate seamlessly with the business's current infrastructure, reducing the complexity of managing the storage environment.

To ensure the successful implementation of a Fiber Channel SAN, SMBs should also plan for ongoing monitoring and management. While Fiber Channel networks are known for their high reliability, regular monitoring and maintenance are still necessary to keep the system running smoothly. SMBs should implement automated monitoring tools that can track the performance of the network, identify potential issues before they become critical, and alert administrators to any problems. Regular performance reviews and health checks can help ensure that the SAN continues to meet the business's evolving data storage needs. Additionally, as the business grows and storage needs increase, SMBs should plan for periodic upgrades to ensure that the SAN remains scalable and capable of handling additional data.

Finally, SMBs should carefully plan for disaster recovery and data backup. Although Fiber Channel SANs offer high availability and fault tolerance, having a solid disaster recovery plan in place is crucial to mitigate the risk of data loss due to hardware failures, natural disasters, or cyberattacks. By implementing regular data backups, both on-site and off-site, and testing the recovery process, SMBs can ensure that their data remains protected and recoverable in the event of an emergency. Fiber Channel SANs can be integrated with backup solutions that ensure fast and reliable recovery, minimizing downtime and ensuring business continuity.

Implementing a Fiber Channel network for SMBs requires thoughtful planning, careful consideration of costs and infrastructure, and an understanding of the business's current and future storage needs. By selecting the right components, securing the network, and implementing best practices for performance, security, and disaster recovery, SMBs can create a scalable, high-performance storage environment that supports their growth and business objectives.

# Case Studies of Successful Fiber Channel and SAN Implementations

Fiber Channel and Storage Area Networks (SANs) have become integral to modern data center infrastructures, offering high-performance, low-latency, and scalable storage solutions. While large enterprises have long adopted these technologies, small and medium-sized businesses (SMBs) and various industries are increasingly realizing the benefits of Fiber Channel SANs. The implementation of such networks often presents challenges, but when done effectively, Fiber Channel and SAN solutions can significantly enhance data access, storage efficiency, and overall operational performance. Exploring case studies of successful Fiber Channel and SAN implementations can provide valuable insights into how organizations have leveraged these technologies to meet their data storage and management needs, and how others can replicate similar successes.

One of the most notable examples of a successful Fiber Channel SAN implementation comes from a large healthcare organization that needed to modernize its data storage infrastructure to handle growing patient data volumes. Prior to the implementation, the organization relied on direct-attached storage (DAS) and a basic network-attached storage (NAS) solution that lacked the speed and scalability required to support increasing data access demands. This resulted in slow data retrieval times, delays in accessing critical patient information, and increased risk of data loss due to the limitations of their storage systems. To address these challenges, the organization turned to a Fiber Channel SAN solution, which enabled faster data transfer speeds, higher availability, and robust fault tolerance capabilities.

The implementation involved deploying high-performance storage arrays connected through a dedicated Fiber Channel network, which facilitated high-speed data access and efficient data management across the organization. The system was designed with redundancy in mind, ensuring that if one path or device failed, data would still be accessible through another. This design was particularly important in healthcare, where patient data must be available at all times to support medical professionals in making timely decisions. The implementation not only improved performance and reduced downtime but also allowed the organization to scale its storage infrastructure as patient data continued to grow. Additionally, the centralized nature of the SAN enabled better data management and backup strategies, leading to a significant reduction in data retrieval times and improved compliance with regulatory requirements such as HIPAA.

In the financial sector, a global banking institution faced challenges with managing large volumes of transactional data while maintaining high performance and security. The bank's legacy storage systems were not able to keep up with the ever-increasing demands of high-frequency trading, real-time analytics, and transaction processing. These performance issues led to slow transaction times, which could potentially impact the bank's competitiveness in the market. To address this, the bank implemented a Fiber Channel SAN to support its mission-critical applications, which required both high speed and low latency.

The implementation of the SAN was designed to support massive data throughput while providing a secure and reliable data storage environment. By utilizing Fiber Channel's high-speed connectivity, the bank was able to dramatically reduce transaction times, ensuring that all data transactions were processed in real-time. Moreover, the bank took advantage of the SAN's scalability, allowing it to expand its storage capacity as needed without major disruptions to operations. The increased efficiency and speed of the SAN solution resulted in significant cost savings and improved performance for trading systems, contributing to the bank's competitive edge in the market. Additionally, the SAN architecture ensured high availability and security, critical elements for maintaining financial transactions and compliance with industry regulations.

A third example of successful Fiber Channel and SAN implementation comes from a major retail company that needed to improve the efficiency and reliability of its e-commerce platform. The company's existing storage solutions were struggling to support the increasing number of online orders and product data, causing slow website performance, delayed order processing, and customer dissatisfaction. The retailer chose to implement a Fiber Channel SAN to improve the speed of its e-commerce transactions and ensure that product data was accessible in real-time.

The implementation involved a dedicated Fiber Channel SAN infrastructure that connected the e-commerce servers, inventory management systems, and product databases. This allowed the retailer to access product information, process orders, and update inventory levels quickly and without interruptions. With the high-speed connectivity provided by Fiber Channel, the retailer was able to reduce latency, ensuring that website data was loaded in real-time, and customers experienced a seamless online shopping experience. Additionally, the SAN allowed for better data redundancy and backup capabilities, ensuring that customer information and transaction records were securely stored and protected from data loss. The retailer also saw improvements in inventory management, as the centralized storage solution allowed for more accurate and up-to-date product tracking, which ultimately led to better decision-making and reduced stockouts.

Another noteworthy case comes from a research university that needed to handle large datasets for scientific research and analysis. The university's research departments were generating and processing massive amounts of data from experiments, simulations, and genomic studies. The existing storage infrastructure, which relied on DAS and a simple NAS setup, was struggling to provide the speed and capacity required to manage these vast datasets. As a result, the university faced long wait times for data access, slow processing speeds, and inefficiencies in managing the storage environment.

To address these challenges, the university implemented a Fiber Channel SAN to provide high-speed, centralized data storage for its research teams. The SAN was configured to support both primary and archival storage, with high-performance storage arrays used for active research data and more cost-effective storage solutions used for long-term data storage. The centralized SAN allowed researchers to quickly access data and collaborate on large-scale projects, enhancing productivity and accelerating the pace of scientific discovery. Moreover, the university benefited from improved data security and compliance with research data management standards, as the SAN architecture ensured that data was securely stored, regularly backed up, and easily recoverable in the event of a failure.

In the manufacturing sector, a global automotive company faced challenges related to the growing complexity of its design and engineering data. The company's product development teams were working with large, complex datasets, including 3D models, simulation data, and design specifications. The legacy storage systems used by the company were not capable of providing the high-performance data access required for these data-intensive applications, leading to delays in product development and inefficiencies in collaboration across teams.

The company implemented a Fiber Channel SAN to centralize its storage environment and ensure that design and engineering teams could access the data they needed in real-time. The SAN allowed for seamless data sharing and collaboration, ensuring that teams could work on the most current versions of designs and simulations. The high-speed data transfer capabilities of the SAN ensured that large design files could be accessed and edited without lag, significantly improving workflow efficiency. Additionally, the SAN's reliability and fault tolerance features ensured that the company's data was protected, reducing the risk of data loss and ensuring that product development could continue without interruption.

These case studies highlight the versatility and effectiveness of Fiber Channel and SAN solutions across various industries. Whether it's improving data access for healthcare organizations, reducing latency in financial institutions, enhancing e-commerce transactions for retailers, supporting research data management at universities, or streamlining collaboration in manufacturing, Fiber Channel SANs offer scalable, high-performance solutions that meet the unique needs of businesses. Each of these organizations was able to address its specific storage challenges through the implementation of a Fiber Channel

SAN, leading to improved performance, greater reliability, and increased efficiency. By learning from these examples, other organizations can better understand how Fiber Channel SANs can help them solve their own data management and storage challenges, ultimately leading to more streamlined operations and greater success.

www.ingramcontent.com/pod-product-compliance
Lightning Source LLC
Chambersburg PA
CBHW071150050326
40689CB00011B/2053